What Readers are Saying About *The Green Velvet Chair*

"What's the definition of a badass? Someone who is tough, uncompromising, and intimidating. Laura Ballerini, the author of *The Green Velvet Chair*, is two-thirds badass. Read her book to find out which two. Through her collection of essays in her debut book, Ballerini invites us to experience how art and design can influence everyday life. With personal reflections that will make you laugh and cry, Ballerini recounts her early days as a designer for a big city newspaper, shares worldly travel anecdotes and family tales that we can all relate to."

– Allison McGee

"Ballerini's writing style is excellent. Engaging. Each word and paragraph draw me to the next word and paragraph. The images that her words create are vivid. The stories are wonderful. I didn't know about The Sphere in New York City that stood between the North and South Towers. I looked it up, and I loved the sculpture and the story behind it. I also didn't know what a Callery Pear tree was and the incredible story behind it. This piece is amazing. "

– Jeff Nelson, President, Anduro Marketing

"The timeliness of the pandemic stories made the book very current, and these chapters resonated deeply with me. Another aspect of the book was that Laura's "work" was blended into every aspect of her life…She isn't a designer for 8 hours, then goes home and becomes a 'non-designer.' Laura is a designer through and through. Her creativity doesn't stop when the workday is over."

– Caran Magaw, Artist

"Loved the Graceland and Red Crayon chapters. I could feel Laura's anxiety coming off the page. I connected with that feeling of not being in control."

– Dana Goldstein, Author of *Murder on My Mind*

"The storyteller hits it straight on. Sharing her life stories brings us to a place of our own. We can truly see the passion Laura Ballerini brings to the page of her life experiences with humour, compassion, creativity, and love. LOVE to read "real life" stories that I can relate to. I enjoyed each chapter as it exploded with a different story. Tying each precious chapter into her work as a designer brings the stories to life. I think we can all find a chapter or two that will bring us back to the 'good ole days'!"

– Brenda Sevick

"An original piece of art. Laura Ballerini generously shares her experiences in life. She has described her experiences of art and design in a most unique way. Heartwarming stories of her and her loved one's creativity and talents. The artist is a gifted individual who is able to capture her audiences with her storytelling. She conveys touching tales about her mother and mother-in-law. Having known them personally, I would say they were described to perfection. I could clearly see the green velvet chair and the smoking. In fact, I have seen both. The green velvet chair is a true testimony of the writer's mother. This book immortalized hard work, dedication, and perfection, which, simply put, is Laura's greatest creative self. And yes, she is a BADASS."

– Lindsay Walters

THE GREEN VELVET CHAIR

Green Velvet Chair

Laura Elizabeth Ballerini

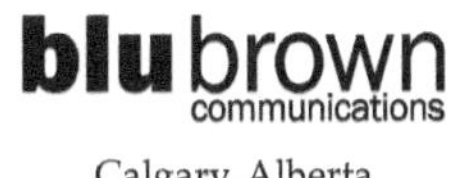

Calgary, Alberta

BluBrown Communications Inc.
Calgary, Alberta, Canada
Email: Info@BluBrown.com

These essays are based on the author's experiences as she recalls them. The names, dates, and details are based on her accounts. While we have made every effort to accurately convey any historical dates and circumstances, this is not an official reference of any kind, and the author and publisher waive any liability to events or persons referenced herein.

First Edition: January 2022
Second Edition: The Green Velvet Chair 2025

Jacket photograph copyright © 2025 by Laura E. Ballerini
Design by Laura E. Ballerini
Cover photography by Laura E. Ballerini
Author photography by Riverwood Photography
Book layout by Hollow Arrow Design
Editor, Kathy Sparrow, Founder & CEO of A Writable Life

Softcover ISBN 978-1-0689895-0-6
Hardcover ISBN 978-1-0689895-1-3
E-book ISBN 978-1-0689895-2-0

Ordering information:
Special discounts are available on quantity
purchases by corporations, associations, and others.
For details, contact info@BluBrown.com

Dedication

To my mother who inspired me, my father who encouraged me,
my blue and brown-eyed daughters who gave me the gift of
motherhood, and to my dear husband who has always believed in me.

"I think everything in life is art. What you do. How you dress. The way you love someone, and how you talk. Your smile and your personality. What you believe in, and all your dreams. The way you drink your tea. How you decorate your home. Or party. Your grocery list. The food you make. How your writing looks. And the way you feel.

Life is art."

— *Helena Bonham Carter*

Contents

Foreword

I've had the absolute joy of knowing Laura Ballerini since our youthful days together in the *Calgary Herald* Advertising Department. I was one of those pesky sales reps coming to her with client requests to "add a starburst" or jam more copy into the beautiful expanse of white space in a thoughtfully created ad. Laura was always patient and gracious in her rejection of such graphically mortifying changes and provided me with compelling rationale that would ultimately win over even the most stubborn of clients. There was lots of laughter in those encounters, me knowing I was being outrageous, Laura knowing she could convince me that the dreaded starburst might have its place, but it certainly wasn't in that particular ad.

We've both moved along since those days, each of us ending up as independent business owners—mine a more convoluted path than Laura's. Staying connected, sharing stories. And each of us becoming writers.

Because I can be a little obsessive about research, I've read a lot of books about writing. A lot. One of my favourites is Natalie Goldberg's *Writing Down the Bones*. In it, Goldberg tells us to "say a holy yes to the real things of our life as they exist." *The Green Velvet Chair* is Laura's "holy yes."

In this delightful and vulnerable collection of stories, Laura shows the same patient and graceful approach to the many characters that appear on the pages as she did with me in my ad-design demands.

Her stories provoke tears and laughter and allow us as readers to find ourselves in her awkward moments of jealousy and her painful stretches of great loss. We participate in the creation of her family's exotic and fairy-tale costumes, and in the chain-gang flower-making production of her eldest daughter's elegant wedding. Along the way, Laura coaxes us into an understanding of the beauty and necessity of complementary colours, of the critical requirement of exactly the right choice of fabric, and of the artistry poured into the creation of a traditional Italian Christmas Eve dish made on a table that has perfectly fit its purpose for generations. We sit in the treasured green velvet chair as we learn of its farmer's field origin and the painstaking refurbishing under the loving hands of a woman of vision.

Her stories shine with the love of her craft and of her family.

Whether we look at the world from a cat's vantage point or wonder at the value of one red crayon, these stories will expand our understanding of the role of design in our world and in our personal relationships. Laura takes us on a journey filled with characters both poignant and hilarious and wraps it all up in a bow made beautiful with intricate details and observation.

I read this book often rippling with laughter, and sometimes through a sheen of heartbroken tears. Laura's words touched my heart and have given me new insight into the finer points of design theory told through allegory. You won't even notice you're being schooled; she is so masterful.

This book will have you looking at your world through thoughtful, focused designer's eyes. And, with any luck, it will give you endless reasons to see how that world of yours makes absolute sense.

– **Kimberlee Jones**, APR,
Author of *The Night Sky Cries* and contributor to *Uncommon Grounds,* a poetry anthology by the Espresso Poetry Collective

Preface

Let's Try this Again

Like a home reno, the second edition of *The Green Velvet Chair* includes some new stories and a refreshed cover design. After recently renewing my love of designing Barbie doll clothes, I have added new chapters titled ***I'm Sew in Love with Barbie, A Day at the Museum,*** and ***Designer Genes,*** which all connect generations together through art and design. These additions round out my recent activities. They tell stories about me finding my long-lost passion again, and also sharing stories of my granddaughter's adventures in art. I bring lessons from both my work and daily life. Additionally, an epilogue introduces a new project. There is a preview of future stories in the epilogue, and I plan to add many positive, inspiring, and life-changing stories within it.

Now, here's the reason for the second edition.

You see, the first edition of *The Green Velvet Chair* was written during COVID-19, completed during a surprise diagnosis of breast cancer, and quietly launched during my cancer treatment. Some may say this was bad luck, but I say it happened the way it was supposed to.

Now I'm giving my stories new life with additional chapters —chapters enhanced with renewed energy and even greater sensitivity to the art and design that surrounds us. As Kim Jones says in the Foreword, this is truly my "holy yes" to the real things of my life as they exist. A breast cancer diagnosis changes you as you navigate life through healing eyes. While it is still written through a creative lens, these new additions focus on the trials and tribulations of realizing your mortality and moving forward with renewed creativity and determination.

How have I changed? Today, I am stronger, smarter, and more sagacious.

Two years ago, I was soldiering up, hunkering down, and plowing through. I was in the trenches with biopsies, surgeries, chemotherapy, radiation—and, of course, a shiny new bald head.

After being diagnosed with breast cancer, many told me: "If you're going to have cancer, breast cancer is the best one to have. It gets the most funding, treatment advancements, and best prognosis."

Some people even said, "Oh, you got the sexy cancer!"

One of my oldest friends had the audacity to tell me, "Your cancer treatment was a cakewalk compared to mine!"

But there was one friend, a cancer survivor, too, who warned me of the hazards to come. She frequently touched base, encouraged me, and informed me of the upcoming perils. She also shared strategies to maneuver through them. Her own cancer journey was very long, arduous, and harrowing. She is one of my heroes. *Thank you, Allison.*

When I initially wrote *The Green Velvet Chair*, I had playfully coined myself "Badass Ballerini," but I never thought I would use it as a badge of honour to battle cancer. However, I focused on the fact that many people before me had fought cancer—and so could I.

I saw all the positives and didn't focus on the negatives.

I was brave for my family—especially my husband, who was devastated by the diagnosis. His devastation turned to bitterness and anger as he could not comprehend how his wife could be stricken with cancer. My husband has always been touched (*or maybe frustrated*) by my incessant drive to always do the right thing—in every aspect of life —from caring for his ailing mother over many years to simply holding the door open for someone. In his eyes, he felt there was nothing fair about such a good person becoming a cancer victim. The thing is, life is not fair, and I honestly never thought of myself as a victim. I saw it as yet another challenge to overcome, and I took it in stride. Determination got me through the process, as many other cancer patients before and after me will do.

Yet, after the treatments came the side effects. I did not see some of them coming.

The hair.

I kept telling myself: "It's only hair."

But it was such a big part of me. I still mourn the loss of my hair as it obstinately regrows. It's coming in slowly. It is thick and coarse and oh so white. I've been dying my hair since my thirties, so when I looked in the mirror, I didn't recognize the person looking back at me. She was an old lady with short, coarse, gray hair. Curly, unruly, tenacious locks that stuck up at the crown—and a stubborn cowlick that defied gravity!

The skin.

What happened to my smooth, ivory skin? It was marred with sores. And although hair wasn't growing on my head very quickly, it was growing on my face. Thick, dark hair appeared as sideburns below my ear lobes. My chin was lush with fine, white hair!

Due to some unusual circumstance, my hands were covered in lesions that displayed varying degrees of healing. They were sore and painful. What was going on!

The visible and invisible side effects of aggressive treatments were starting to show.

The depression.

"You can be sad. You can go there. But you can't stay there." ~ Heather Jose

Now, I understand the meaning of PTSD. When you are in "the battle," you focus on survival. You do what you need to do to stay alive. You attend to the functions of the day, while hoping to reach the end game. I masked the journey with a brave smile and a positive attitude.

But now I am asking myself, "What the hell just happened?

I reflected on what some people said to me upon my diagnosis. "You got the 'sexy cancer.'" "Your cancer journey was a 'cakewalk' compared to mine." Who says stuff like this?

Any challenge—whether physical or mental—is hard. We shouldn't play it down, suppress it, or pretend it doesn't matter. *It Does Matter. We All Matter!*

I learned that we need to support each other no matter what challenge we are going through—without judgment.

The outlook.

It is better each day.

I have met angels along the way (many in the healthcare system).

My hair is long, newly styled, and dyed. I have learned to tame my disorderly tresses.

My skin is healed, and the lesions are gone. The only scars are in my mind.

My body is lighter and healthier in so many ways as I exercise and move every day—grateful for this!

My mind is overcoming the trauma of the last few years, and I feel like I am finally coming out the other side! I have joined support groups. I have listened, shared, acknowledged, and respected the journey others have gone through. I have met warriors who have survived their own combat zones…

I learned to crawl through my battlefield until I could finally dance and celebrate each personal victory along the way.

While I wrote the first edition spurred on by my dad through the years —*and a wish that he would finally get to read it curled up on a soft cloud in heaven*—it's with a heavy heart that my journey now includes a breast cancer storyline.

On the anniversary of my cancer treatments, this second edition seemed appropriate, but bittersweet. I hope you enjoy the fresh, positive chapters as well as those stories that ferociously challenged me.

Introduction

The Green Velvet Chair

Sometimes Inspiration Comes from the Most Unlikely Places

As a child, I remember when Mom bought an old, dilapidated armchair from a farmer. It sat threadbare and shabby amongst the weeds in his field. But Mom saw something special in it. Much to my dad's chagrin, Mom excitedly carted it home with plans to restore it. My father, siblings, and I thought, *oh dear, what's Mom going to do with this piece of junk?*

But she had a vision that none of us saw. I explain more about Mom and this chair in Chapter 2, but here's a bit of the story.

Mom stripped that chair down to its horsehair stuffing and basic wooden frame, discarding the tattered outer layers. I think she soon realized that she may have bitten off more than she could chew. But true to her unwavering style, she promptly enrolled in an upholstery course. In class, the walnut arms and legs were sanded down, stained, and varnished to perfection. She then re-tied the springs and bought firm, new foam, and elegant upholstery fabric. She recovered the chair, detailing the back with deep, diamond tufts. She finished off the design with covered buttons placed at the base of each tuft and a new bottom cushion edged with crisp piping.

What fabric did she choose? A rich, green velvet.

Today, as the green velvet chair sits audaciously in front of my window, the sun shines on the still-luxurious fabric, with soft shadows accenting the deep diamond design. Each day I look at it and appreciate the power of vision, the ability to implement a vision, and most importantly, the tenacity to plough through when others don't see your vision.

It also taught me to look at art and design in a new light—each day, every day.

And that's what I wanted to share when I wrote this book.

I Found My Voice and Got Lost in Words

I am a quiet and introverted creative. When I told people I was writing a book, many of them were surprised and asked me why. Apparently, I must have seemed like an unlikely candidate to put pen to paper—and to be honest, I even surprised myself.

Like many people, I often felt like I was not being heard. While in a networking session, a meeting, or even a family dinner, I struggled to enter into the conversation. I even had nightmares about losing my voice and being unable to talk or yell for help.

But somewhere along the way, I took a business book writing workshop and subsequently signed up for classes. While I didn't want to write a book about my business per se, I did want to write about something that I knew—art and design. After a year or so of working with the writing coach, I engaged a second coach who taught me the fine art of oral storytelling. This was how I gained confidence and found my true passion around telling stories.

Sharing my stories verbally to a captive audience made me realize that my experiences resonated with others. And with the encouragement of my coach, I started to write short essays about art and design in everyday life. This is a collection of many of them.

CHAPTER 1

From Picas to Pixels and Beyond

Let's Start at the Beginning

For most of my adult life as a graphic designer, I have been counting pixels. But early in my career, I was counting picas. Most people today have never heard of a pica.

A pica is a unit of measure used in the print publishing world. I started my career in advertising, working as a designer for a big-city newspaper. It was the heyday of the publishing world in the 80s and 90s.

I loved my job in Creative Services, which functioned as a mini design agency for the newspaper. The advertising department was an exciting place to be. It was made up of a great team of designers—each of them had their own style and personality, which made the experience all the more interesting. The newspaper was a progressive, equal-opportunity employer, and our department was made up of both men and women from varying backgrounds, including some from different countries. Most of the team had degrees in Visual Communications, but some designers were self-taught and extremely talented. The diversity of our team made us stronger.

One talented designer moved all the way from Germany to Canada. *The Calgary Stampede* brought him here and working at the newspaper allowed him to pursue his boyhood dream—to become a real-live cowboy. He was enthralled with western culture and quickly became a full-fledged, trick-roping cowboy. He was equally enchanted with the Indigenous Peoples culture and gathered a precious collection of memorabilia from his First Nation friends garnered over many years. Each *Stampede Week*, he brought his horse onto the green space framing our outdoor breakfast area and entertained the newspaper staff. Standing on the saddle of his horse, he performed complex rope maneuvers to a cheering crowd.

Entertained by The Crown

Another fellow designer, who was an outrageous flirt with the ladies, went on to become a world-famous artist swept up by George Lucas of *Star Wars* fame. He later became an official illustrator for Disney Studios. This fellow was an English gentleman with an outlandish sense of humour. I have many memories of his shenanigans that mostly happened when we were working late. At Christmastime, our department worked a lot of overtime, as retailers ran several additional ads over this lucrative buying season.

One night this fellow designer (*trying to energize our tired department*), emerged from the bathroom dressed up as the Queen of England. I kid you not—wig, fur stole, gold lame dress, topped with a jewel encrusted crown and sturdy-heeled shoes. He loved to get a rise out of us and never failed to have us in stitches. Comic relief in its purest form.

On that evening, there was a group of school children being heralded through the building for a guided tour of the newspaper. We were mortified when they saw my co-worker wandering the halls masquerading as Queen Elizabeth herself. However, it further added to the silliness of the evening. *I still wonder what those kids told their parents when they got home.*

While there were many hilarious moments like this one, looking back, the newspaper industry was often a rigorous boot camp for designing under the toughest of conditions. Many designers went on to do their best work beyond the boundaries of the Creative Services department.

Like all revenue-generating businesses, this too was sales-oriented, and the sales department was the driving force behind the newspaper industry. Advertising, after all, supported the real talent within the newspaper business—the journalists.

We were producing a new product every day. Our readers purchased the paper to read the world-class reporting printed on its pages. It was framed with ads that drove revenue and enabled the business to flourish.

This job was life-changing for me. Having just become a mother to my first daughter, I started this new position with great anticipation. It was not only a good career move, but it also housed one of the first corporate daycares in the city. I got to be part of a big machine that churned out a high-quality product on a daily basis. And on top of it all, I could see my daughter playing outside on the grass with the other employees' children. As the years went by, people would ask my daughter what her mom did at the newspaper, and she would say: "My mommy colours all day!" Hard to believe the days before computers ever existed—when we designed with felt markers and paper!

The advertising department was made up of several services—arguably, sales being the most important, but also included design, production, and sales support. Our department was important to the sales teams who worked closely with us to develop strong ads for clients to purchase. Our designs, after all, helped the reps make their sales quotas. On a good day, our department would lay out hundreds of ads at a time. The ads ranged from full-page, full-colour automotive ads chock full of starbursts and buying incentives, to quarter-page black and white ads designed for the high-end shoe company who demanded page-three positioning, *(which was the most coveted spot in our daily paper)*.

The ads were filled to the brim with images and copy. White space was perceived as wasted space. In contrast, designers saw white space as "breathing room." Nevertheless, clients thought that by filling every pica with content they would get their money's worth from the much sought-after ad space. Prices were based on circulation (*as well as colour, position, and day of the week*), so we brazenly bragged about our high subscription base, as it had a direct correlation to the number of eyeballs that would see the ads.

Managing the Clients (or not)

Our clients were a cast of characters, some of whom bypassed their sales rep and swooped into our department for direct creative assistance. They'd eagerly bring their ideas into our department trying to find a designer at the rows of drafting desks who would make eye contact with them. We would spot the rogue client from the corner of our eyes but kept our heads down trying to get our current workload completed by deadline. Oftentimes, the sales rep would chase their client down, steer them back to the boardroom and reel in the account. It was a constant balancing act of managing client expectations with what we could deliver in an already unrealistic turnaround time.

More often than not, ads slipped through the cracks and copy ran amok, sometimes creating the most humorous typos. One automotive client was having a tent sale on the weekend. Rather than the heading saying, "Find out what's under Mike's tarp" (*as it was supposed to*), it read "Find out what's under Mike's trap"—that typo still makes me laugh out loud, especially when you think about the reputation some car salespeople had back then.

Ads were flying out the door at any given time, with sales reps racing in and out to make deadline. Those were the days before cell phones, email, or the Internet. Fax machines were just being introduced. Sales reps were on the ground running, meeting clients in their set territories, selling, presenting, and revising ads at record speed. Upon approval, we had to lay out the ads and pass them on to the composing room. This was essentially the production department. They took our felt marker design layouts and built them as camera-ready artwork using wax—yes, wax—to hold it all together. Unlike glue, wax could be lifted and repositioned, because ad revisions were plentiful. Deadlines were everyone's priority. The pace was fast and the clients demanding, making it a great training ground for a fast-paced career in design.

The '88 Winter Olympics were definitely the highlight of my newspaper days. It was an exciting time to be "in the centre of it all." We had the opportunity to have our work seen by the world. We also had the privilege of placing gorgeous ads in our newspaper created by leading ad agencies from various countries. The eyes of the world were on our city, and it was a magical time to be in the media.

Collaboration at its Finest

Looking back on my newspaper days, I realized what a tight, cohesive team we were. Creative services, sales, composing, and sales support were a well-oiled machine. We were a mix of every personality you could imagine but somehow, we bonded and amalgamated into probably the best team I have ever worked in. Days were jam-packed with deadlines involving last-minute changes from clients, and sales reps clamouring to get their ads completed before the other reps came in. The pressure was intense as we all wanted to make sure our daily product was as flawless and effective as possible. High expectations created such an incredible energy within the building that each night I went home, I was incredibly proud of my day's work—and incredibly tired.

Since those newspaper days, I have progressed through the design world in what, at times, seemed like lightning speed, but never with the fierce camaraderie experienced there. Although I'm still catching my breath from a whirlwind career, my heart often beckons me back to the "good old days" at the newspaper. But while those days are long gone, they set me up for bigger adventures.

Movin' On

Since leaving the paper publication business decades ago, I have moved from counting picas to counting pixels and beyond. I followed my newspaper boss, whom I had great respect for, into the brave new world of websites. In the early 90s we were designing some of the first websites in the city. *Boy, am I dating myself!* But looking back, it was quite revolutionary.

I took a huge risk in leaving a stable, well-paying job at the newspaper to delve into the great unknown world of the Internet and all things digital. I was designing interactive CD-ROMs enhanced with audio, video, and databases developed by high-end, bleeding-edge programmers. It was exciting and the learning curve was steep.

Now, here I am, running my own boutique design agency many decades later.

While I learned to count picas and then pixels, I am now counting impressions and monitoring conversion rates. The days of cutting out a coupon from a newspaper and sending it in, with a marketing department somewhere compiling the results, are of a bygone era. As a designer, I now get to conduct A/B testing with ads (*simply put, designing two very unique advertising campaigns*) to monitor which one gets more clicks, more forms submitted, and more sales. Real-time analytics have changed the design world and made me much more responsive to what works and what doesn't. Being reactive and responsive helps to hone my creative skills and forces me to "digitally listen" to the target audience(s).

The world of design has evolved, and I am proud to have grown and learned so much along the way. But throughout this digital learning, I still pick up a pencil from time to time and draw—usually portraits of my children and grandchildren. And to my utter surprise, my children, who grew up with the Internet, are fascinated with my hand drawings.

And as I reconnect with my co-workers from the newspaper industry through social media, I am astonished (*but not surprised*) by the creativity that abounds from them. Former sales reps have become successful painters, voice artists, poets, and writers. Fellow creative services designers have become flourishing jewelry artists, quilters, painters, and photographers, including as mentioned, a famous Disney artist. I have come to appreciate that the fast-paced, high-pressure world of advertising sales and design instilled a very creative passion in many of us. Perhaps that is what dreams are made of—looking for the next opportunity to grow and soar.

From picas to pixels—and beyond.

CHAPTER 2

Watching My Mother Through the Smoke

Green Velvet Soon Turned to Grey Ash

My mother was a heavy smoker. One after another throughout the day, she skillfully balanced a cigarette between her yellow-stained index and middle fingers. Frequently, it burned in a nearby ashtray as she knitted, sewed, or worked on an elaborate petit point. As she worked, her cylindrical companion frequently rested in an ashtray overflowing with butts—the grey cinders falling softly around it. Silently, with covert maneuvers, this grey ash would slowly overtake her body, but we didn't see it coming—yet.

As kids, we tried to avoid the ashtray when the cigarette smoke was rising from it. The fumes scorched the hairs in our tiny nostrils. My brother, in particular, had great disdain for these white, tar-ridden chambers. But they gave my mom comfort. As a young child, I could see when she took a deep puff she relaxed and briefly closed her eyes.

And even with this addictive habit clouding her presence, I have dedicated this chapter to my mom because she was the single-most influential person in my life. The most creative person I ever met. She was as tough as she was talented. Though she was not one to hug any of her four children or make a fuss about their day, we felt loved. She was my inspiration and unquestionably the reason I chose to go to art college and become a designer.

My mother was an artist of fabrics and wool and embroidery thread (*and so much more*). She was a magnificent talent. You could ask anyone who met her, and they would say the same thing.

Art and design were woven through our daily lives growing up, and impacted our family significantly. Oddly enough, I think the smoke breaks she frequently took helped her work through a creative issue—giving her time to develop her critical-thinking skills.

A Burning Desire to Create

Creativity touched our daily lives with my mother delving into one design project after another. She was a force to be reckoned with when it came to creating something from, well, anything, really—textiles, exotic woods, and even food items.

Coming from a Ukrainian background, she had the most incredible patience creating pysanky Easter eggs. She taught her four children this craft, and we painstakingly tried to mimic her elaborate designs. Dot after dot, we tried.

Good Friday was the day we all spent hovering around the stove with the hot wax and our rudimentary kistkas (*a drawing tool filled with hot wax)*. After some shaky designs, we would dip our eggs into coloured water and repeat the process with more wax and more colours.

Needless to say, blobs of wax would inadvertently fall onto the egg and ruin our well-intentioned designs. Some eggs even ended up being thrown into the back alley by my brother out of sheer frustration. *I wonder what the people walking down the alley thought as a dreadful, wax-covered egg came flying by.*

Through the years our skills improved, and my mom began to purchase better dyes from the local Ukrainian store. Vibrant colours came in foil-lined packages that we mixed in individual coffee cups filled with boiling water (*with some colours requiring a tablespoon of vinegar*). We also used better quality bees wax and more modern kistkas to give us greater control of our designs.

Mom, however, always created the best array of eggs, intricately designed in colours brighter than a garden of tulips. Her eggs were coveted and became the centrepiece of our Easter Sunday dinner table.

Recently, my daughters gifted me with an electric kistka which heats the wax to a consistent temperature. This ensures a steady flow of wax with no more blobs. It came with a variety of tips that allowed me to choose different line weights. This has enabled me to create very intricate, detailed designs. After many decades (*and modern tools*), I think the student may have finally become the master.

Art and Design—Part of Each Holiday

My mother was also a master baker. While her pie crust was magnificent, and her chocolate roll decadent, it was her Christmas shortbread that became her prized accomplishment in the kitchen. *I kid you not—they literally melted in your mouth.* Using a wooden spoon, Mom would expertly hand whip the butter in her white, glass mixing bowl, until it was as light and creamy as a cloud. Once the perfect consistency was reached, she would add dry ingredients until flawlessly blended. This process took many hours—usually while she was watching her favourite TV show, *Perry Mason*, in the evening. Like the Easter eggs, the technique used to make these cookies has been the most challenging to master within our family. Neither my children, nor I, have ever been able to replicate these melting morsels, (*although my sister's shortbread comes close*). They were a true work of art that will go down in our family history as masterpieces.

If Only She Were a Man

A pretty strong feminist from the beginning (*and most likely a frustrated woman who wanted more*), Mom was not intimidated by woodworking, typically defined as "men's work." I remember her saying she wished she could have become a carpenter, as she had so many ideas and projects she wanted to do—*if only she were a man*. Growing up in an era with no gender equality, I think she felt a bit held back, and she hoped for more when her daughters grew up.

Stubbornly, in typical "Mom-fashion," she was always trying to prove herself to the world. Her ideas were grand and sometimes unorthodox—and undoubtedly hard for others to visualize.

I remember the time she found a tired old chair next to remnants of a brass bed found sitting in a farmer's field among the thistles. My father furtively rolled his eyes as Mom went to the farmer and offered him a small amount of money for the old relics. I don't think the farmer took the money from her, as he considered it "junk" and was glad to be rid of it. Dad reluctantly carted the rickety chair and brass bed frame home while his wife excitedly deliberated about her latest projects.

Upon arrival at home, she promptly cleaned the brass, eager to see what would reveal itself under the layers of muck and grime. She worked on it for days and brought it back to its original luxurious sheen. It became the centrepiece of the bedroom I shared with my sister—its ornate molded crown resting on hand-casted horizontal bars.

Mom then evaluated the old chair and promptly enrolled in a furniture refinishing course—complete with upholstery lessons. In her male-dominated classroom, she ripped the old chair down to its horsehair stuffing and worn-out springs. She learned how to re-tie the springs, reinforcing the structure to its original sturdiness. She then examined the scratched walnut arms and legs. The intricately carved pieces were delicately sanded so as not to disturb the original craftsmanship of the engraved wood. Like an artist with a vision, she stained them a deep, rich brown, and then turned to the threadbare upholstery.

A green velvet, mimicking the look and feel of deep moss, was chosen to adorn this throne. Mom, a gifted seamstress, painstakingly stitched the curved bottom cushion with decorative piping around the top and bottom edges. She then masterfully tufted the back of the chair with well-placed diamond mounds. Each diamond was accented with a velvet-covered button placed at the base of each tuft.

None of us kids saw her vision for these two pieces when she dragged them home from the farmer's field, worn down by the weather, the weeds, and the years. But boy, could we appreciate her finished pieces.

While the Farmer Saw Junk, Mom Saw Treasure

The green velvet chair now sits proudly in my home—radiating a kind of arrogant austerity. It has a regal presence all its own. A visitor once commented that the next time he came over, he would wear a smoking jacket, complete with an ascot and the finest Cuban cigar, so he could be worthy of sitting in that chair. This made me appreciate the powerful vision she must have had for this piece. *The influence of art and design—through my mother in her finest hour.*

Sew Creative

Through necessity, my mother sewed all our clothes to help make ends meet. My father worked hard as a purchasing agent for a large steel company, and my mother tried to contribute as a stay-at-home mom in the 1960s. As time went on, her talent flourished, and she became a coveted couturier for all the neighbourhood ladies who were enthralled with her impeccable taste, accurate fittings, and flawless sewing skills. She would tailor the paying ladies' outfits to perfection, creating everything from evening gowns of exquisite brocade and lace, to bright-orange hot pants (*all the rage in the late '60s*). She honed her skills to expertly sew thick, rich velvets with perfect seams (*with no puckers or pulls*), and the neighbourhood ladies kept coming.

I remember my mother in the early years—creating designs from fabrics in her busy sewing room. The room overflowed with stacks of neatly folded fabrics, rows of colourful threads lined up on bolts like soldiers, and a dress form artistically draped in materials—inspiring her next creation. It was exciting to enter her domain and witness such a splendid combination of textures and notions. She had drawers filled to the brim with patterns organized by gender and size. Cabinets housed small bins that were equally organized with zippers, snaps, elastics, and buttons. An astounding display of skill, talent, and passion were on display in this sewing room. It was like a museum of art and design in the making—and it brought me great joy and inspiration.

While the other kids played outside, I hung over my mom's shoulder trying to capture her technique and artful style. I was just a little girl enthralled with watching her sew. It was a time of learning, a time of joy, and a time I treasured.

Looking back, I was almost certainly a distraction to her process, but I wanted to stay and watch, even though she regularly tried to shoo me out. I scrutinized her techniques and learned so much from her. Soon, I was designing and sewing the most elaborate Barbie doll clothes ever seen in the neighbourhood. My Barbie's were the best dressed dolls around. *They mirrored the creations of the paying ladies.* I was learning from the best.

As a hardworking housewife and mother, there came a time when Mom wanted to work outside the house. She went from local neighbourhood seamstress to newly employed factory worker. Once exposed to the commercial sewing industry, her talent was quickly recognized, and she rose to the top. She was swiftly promoted to floor supervisor and then catapulted to head designer of research and development for the international backpack company. She travelled the world, learned more, and shared more. *I truly hope that any person who was lucky enough to work under her sopped up her knowledge the way I had.*

Design was woven throughout my early years by this inspiring woman—although she would be mortified if she read this description of herself. She saw herself as a very humble, hardworking woman, and nothing more. I saw a powerful leader, whose creative design skills influenced everyone around her.

Working in a factory, combined with many years of smoking, took its toll on my mother's lungs. She would never admit it was the smoking, but rather the melting of the webbing materials used in the factory that ruined her health, in combination with that darn cleaning spray she used in the shower. *As you may have suspected, she was also an impeccable housekeeper and her bathroom tiles always shone.* Regardless, the nicotine, the burnt webbing, and the chemicals, forced my mother to quit smoking. She quit because breathing was becoming difficult—a foreshadowing of what was to come.

The day she quit smoking was monumental to our family. It was a big deal, and an event we never thought we would see. My mom loved her cigarettes, and the yellow-stained popcorn ceilings in our house proved it. Shortly after she quit smoking, my brother gave her a very detailed petit point kit to keep her hands busy (*clever young man*). She worked on that picture for almost a year. It was a lovely composition centered around an intricate bouquet of rich, crimson poppies, wispy white daisies, and delicate bluebells, anchored within an ornate vase. It was a complex design with meticulous shadows on the leaves and the flower petals.

For a time, it hung in my bathroom and reflected into a large, mirrored wall. Unwittingly, it created a double-vision of this poignant picture—the last petit point she ever did. I looked at it every day, and while it was beautiful, it made me feel melancholy.

I have often wondered what she must have thought as she stitched each colour into the Penelope canvas (*fabric used for needlepoint*), surrendering the power of those once much-loved cigarettes into this meld of embroidery threads. I suspect they were threads of tears, realizing life was all too short, and changes came too late.

This beautifully designed petit point was a turning point in my mother's life and helped me reflect on unanticipated twists and turns. I have since given this picture to my brother, as it seemed appropriate that he should have it.

My mother suffered a long, slow death over many years. She was diagnosed with emphysema, or COPD, as the doctors called it—a disease that destroyed her lungs and, in the end, forced her to fight for every breath, every day. The doctors gave us a strong visual to describe this disease. They explained that her lungs were originally like "bubble wrap"—filled with little pockets of air. As the disease took over, the pockets of air popped and flattened the lungs so they could no longer inflate with oxygen. A cruel, heartless disease, but a disease provoked (*arguably*) by years of smoking, nonetheless.

In her final years, she succumbed to hauling around an oxygen tank to help her breathe. It weighed down her thin frame and limited the mobility of this once-active woman. I offered to get her a wheelchair so we could go for walks in the park overlooking her home. But she refused, not wanting to be seen being pushed around in a wheelchair. I didn't quite understand this, as it seemed her pride had completely confined her to her home. But it made me realize that her mighty spirit had fallen hard.

She died on a sunny autumn morning, in a remote-controlled bed. The bed was carefully centered in the bay window of her living room, where she could see the birds fly and the children play during recess at the nearby school. Those were her final sights and sounds.

My tribute to her was writing and delivering her eulogy, designing her memorial card, and picking the music that played at the funeral luncheon. While we tried to create some pomp and pageantry around her passing, the irony was she would have wanted a quiet, modest goodbye. Nevertheless, I designed her memorial card adorned with sweet peas (*her favourite flower*) and centred it with a picture of her at a healthier time, wearing a soft grey sweater. The card was framed in dusty rose and embellished with a dainty pink ribbon woven through the base. It was important for me to visually design her funeral to symbolize her creativity and elegance in everything she did.

Many years after her death, I still pay homage to my mother. I aspire to recreate her Ukrainian Easter eggs, follow her recipe for melt-in-your-mouth shortbread, and create the flakiest pie crust I can. Her creative flare also inspires me every day in my design work, across many mediums. As I watched her through the smoke, my own destiny became much clearer.

CHAPTER 3

Digging Deep in the Vatican Museum

How Artwork from the 11th Century Gave Us a Fresh Perspective

Although my husband was born in Italy, George immigrated to Canada with his family at the tender age of three months old. While he still had relatives throughout his homeland, he wasn't an avid traveller, and other life commitments always took precedence over a trip back to his birthplace. However, on the occasion of our 30th wedding anniversary, I was finally able to convince him to take this trip.

We planned to visit his family on the island of Sardinia for the first week, but also wanted to make sure we took in the sights of the rest of the country. So, I booked a bus tour spanning several more weeks. We sought to get the most out of Italy on a comfortable coach, with a tour guide who looked after the logistics. Preparing for our first-ever bus tour, we had the preconceived notion that our fellow passengers would be geriatric—immobile and humdrum.

Our initial jaunt with this group was a one-day tour of Rome, culminating with a dinner excursion 25 kilometers southeast of Rome, in the town of Castel Gandolfo—the location of the Pope's summer residence. The Papal Palace overlooks Lake Albano, a small volcanic crater lake which is one of the focal points of the 17th century villa.

The bus parked at the bottom of the hill, and many of our fellow travellers struggled to walk up the steep knoll to the castle. We had to make several stops along the way, waiting patiently for our slower comrades. Finally, our group made it to the top where we found shops and restaurants within the complex garden paths. While our fellow tourists couldn't keep up with us walking up the hill, they certainly kept up the pace with the drinking and merrymaking at dinner. Everyone's joints and spirits became more limber after lots of wine and an Italian feast of chicken and pasta. Some people even kicked up their heels to the famous Tarantella folk dance.

The restaurant was like a grotto. It had plastic grape leaves and fruit hanging from lattice in the ceiling. While it had a cozy feel, I remember thinking how dusty the fake fruit looked. The walls were painted yellow, and very old, uneven tiles covered the floor. The food and service were excellent, and the live band with its accordion, mandolin, and tambourine created a beautifully cultural occasion. The evening was full of fun and surprises and made us appreciate our new bus buddies as we returned to our awaiting coach.

On this Saturday night in Italy, we were headed back to Rome, chauffeured by our bus driver, Pèpe. When he stood up from his seat, we could see Pèpe was a tall man with a shiny, bald head and a very large frame. He commanded authority. As the boss of the bus, his job was to get us safely from one destination to another.

However, Pèpe was also a playful man with great intuition. He could see that his passengers had loosened up after an evening of frolicking at the Pope's castle. So, for the ride back, he chose some music to entertain the mostly American group, and it wasn't traditional Italian music, as one would think. To our surprise, he played something completely different: *Saturday Night Fever*!

While my husband gravitated to the brooding sounds of Pink Floyd and Black Sabbath, he also loved the disco era. *Weird, I know.*

Saturday Night Fever was one of his favourite soundtracks. In his younger days, my hubby was somewhat of a party animal. However, over the years, he had become rather stodgy. I was his shy, quiet wife who usually hid safely in the background. *I've changed a bit too, allowing my badass to shine from time to time.*

As Pèpe turned up the music and hit the gas pedal, the excitement on the bus accelerated as well. To my shock, my husband jumped up from his seat. He popped up the collar on his black leather jacket and started line dancing down the aisle of the bus, confidently mimicking Travolta's moves. He was a master at the *Brooklyn Shuffle* and was cheered on by an excited group of fans! As he danced up and down the aisle, I sat low in the seat with my arms and legs crossed and blushed slightly with embarrassment. However, soon my husband was joined by an enthusiastic crowd of fellow party animals. Everyone was dancing to the Bee Gees back to Rome. Saturday night fever had begun.

We quickly became the party starters (*well, my husband did*), and everyone wanted to know our names. I replied "We are George and Laura—like the Bushes. You either like us or you don't." They laughed. We think they liked us.

Many in this group became our lifelong friends—from the UK to New York to Australia. And we were forever known as "The Bushes."

Two Days Earlier

We arrived in Rome a couple of days before our tour was to start, as we wanted to feel the pulse of the city on our own before the flurry of the tour began. Our first adventure was to explore St. Peter's Basilica and the Vatican Museums.

St. Peter's Basilica was lavish, but it was also sombre with its crypts and grottos, the holiest being St. Peter's tomb. The architecture, sculptures, and mosaics were overwhelming for me. Years earlier, I studied these masterpieces in the one-dimensional photos of my art history books. And on that day, I felt dwarfed in their presence. From flowing fabric skillfully carved out of a block of stone, to intricately cut glass, I experienced a sense of privilege to have viewed these classic treasures in all their glory. It took me decades to get here, and I savoured every detail.

Construction of the original Basilica began in the year 324 AD, commissioned by Constantine himself. It took centuries to build, and involved many restorations over thousands of years. Art and faith collided in its renaissance and baroque architecture.

I can't recount the entire history of St. Peter's Basilica (*as there are many history books on this topic*). But I will say, I was humbled by the sheer size and scope of this cathedral and somewhat intimidated by the important artists who touched every aspect of this consecrated structure.

With Emperor Constantine's original Basilica crumbling from lack of maintenance, the strong-willed Pope Julius II demanded it be rebuilt. He challenged the miserly

Michelangelo to resurrect the decomposing building into the Renaissance masterpiece it is today. The restoration project took far longer than Michelangelo could personally oversee and was completed from 1506-1626.

I also learned that all the paintings within the Basilica are not actually paintings—they are mosaics. Minuscule, interlocking pieces of coloured glass are arranged to create such detailed images that they appear to be painted with a brush. Much like a fine jigsaw puzzle, they are meticulously arranged shapes to convey a seamless array of light, colour, and story.

During our tour, we also learned that Michelangelo's *Pietà*, a sculpture carved when he was twenty-four years of age, is protected by bullet-proof glass after being attacked by a man with a hammer in the 1970s. Unfortunately, the man had a mental illness, and during his aggressive barrage of strikes, managed to break Mary's arm and nose. With time and expert artistry, the sculpture was carefully mended back to life. This event underlined the power of art. It moves us in different ways—both good and bad.

Our tour of the Vatican Museums and St. Peter's Basilica were unexpectedly emotional. The historical events within the Basilica kept us grounded within our Catholic roots, and our respect for the church became stronger.

The museums were more academic and filled with masterpieces collected by various Popes throughout the centuries. We had meandered through many of the twenty-six museums, each housing specific works of art relative to that period. Viewing thousands of sculptures and paintings was overwhelming, and we were getting tired—even with my artistic background, my enthusiasm was waning. With over 70,000 pieces in the collection, we made a pretty good dent, but my husband was ready for a break.

Attempting to escape through an exit in the Gallery of Tapestries, we were confronted by a wall-hanging looming in front of us.

It was a composition of once-vibrant colours, clearly crafted by skilled hands. But the tapestry that covered most of the masonry beneath it conveyed a story that was barbaric.

The tapestry was woven with silk and masterfully designed—but depicted the worst of mankind. We viewed the image of mayhem—a scene of armed soldiers battling mothers trying to protect their children. This story was depicting the biblical story of King Herod who ordered all males under the age of two years old to be slaughtered. Theoretically, the King was trying to kill the new Messiah (*Jesus*), but this order failed, as Jesus ultimately survived. It felt shameful for us to witness this carnage. My husband was appalled by the tapestry, distraught that such a scene could be hanging in one of the world's holiest places. The lighting was low in this area of the museum, but the midday sun was peeking through the small side windows. This cast shadows on the tapestry that created even more drama, more contrast, and more emotion.

My husband became very upset. "This is the Vatican! Why is this hanging here! It is disgusting and goes against everything the church stands for. We need to leave now. I am so disappointed to see this so-called artwork hanging in this museum."

It took me thirty years to get my husband into a museum. I didn't want this to be his first and last visit to one. So, I dug deep, back to my art history days. I had to remember some details from my one-dimensional art history books and try to instill some calm to the situation. Grasping for the right words,

I explained that this artwork did what it was supposed to do. It evoked deep emotion. It affected us in a way we didn't expect. It aroused an anger and a disgust that we didn't necessarily associate with artwork. But this artist was successful in portraying a time in history. Visually, the tapestry told a violent story that was intended to move the audience.

What I described earlier as my one-dimensional history books, gave me a well-rounded conceptual point of view after all.

- Was it depicting a visual story perhaps before the written word was even developed? Possibly.

- Was this any different from reading about this event in a history book or in the Bible? Not sure.

- Was it appropriate to display on the walls of the Vatican?

Perhaps it was not for us to decide.

But what I do know is that the tapestry art touched us that day—in a way that surprised us. It made us think and feel deeper. It expanded our thought processes and made us delve a little more into history and the Bible. It presented a new conversation and helped us to become more critical thinkers.

Much like our erroneous expectation of our tour-bus companions, our leisurely visit to the Vatican Museum surprised us as well. Our minds became more open that day, and our hearts a bit more exposed to different perspectives.

We could have easily left the museum in a huff and offered disgruntled reviews of the visit to others. Instead, the tapestry triggered emotions that made us more self-aware and empathic, not only to the obvious, but also to what lies beneath the surface.

CHAPTER 4

Follow the Bouncing Ball

Witnessing a Sculpture Transition to a Global Icon

In 1999, I was lured to New York City for a web marketing conference. It was my first trip to the Big Apple as well as my first (*and last*) time inside the World Trade Center, which was host to the popular event. The conference was well-attended. People from all over the US and Canada gathered to learn more about online marketing, which, in 1999, was still in its infancy.

At the time, I was the Creative Director for a large telecommunications firm in Alberta and was excited to visit this fascinating city and learn more about the emerging online industry, which I had been involved in for several years. I would take this knowledge back to my team and share the findings of the week-long educational sessions.

Staying at the Hilton Hotel across the street from the World Trade Center made my commute to the conference very convenient. The early morning walk was brisk as I tried to keep up with New Yorkers on the crowded sidewalk.

The streets were flooded with a sea of yellow cabs. I was entertained by a symphony (*or shall I say a cacophony*) of honking horns, screeching breaks, and obscenity-laden discourse from drivers as I waited for the traffic lights to change. It was exciting. But when it was safe to cross the intersection, I became intimidated as I approached the World Trade Center towering in front of me. The twin towers cast a shadow over me, and I became overwhelmed by their size and prominence on the block.

However, I was welcomed to the plaza by a massive bronze sculpture that reflected a thin sliver of intense sunlight. The spherical sculpture stood between the North and South Towers and was anchored with an enormous fountain at its base. *The Sphere* rotated around its own axis. Waves from the water fountain rushed around its base. The sound of the moving water and the rotation of the sculpture were inviting to my eyes and ears and distracted me from the huge mass of the towers. I had learned this 25-foot sculpture had been designed by German artist, Fritz Koenig and was a symbol of world peace and trade. Koenig referred to this cast as his "biggest child," and I was touched that his artwork had become a part of him in such an intimate way—so much so that he considered it one of his offspring.

Koenig's "biggest child" glistened as the morning sun moved into the plaza. I was captivated by its simple, yet powerful, presence. As a new visitor, I was enchanted by the size, colour, and sheen of this artwork. Surrounded by concrete and tall, grey buildings, the golden sphere brought warmth to a visually cold environment. I could see how world peace radiated from it. It was warm and calming, and also served as a distraction from the flurry of activity around it.

Midway through my first day at the conference, I ventured to the outdoor plaza to enjoy some sunshine and absorb the information from the morning sessions. While many people ate their lunch at the base of this sculpture on a beautiful day in May, it astounded me how many other people whizzed around like it was an obstacle in their way. Koenig's creation was installed many decades earlier, and I wondered if it became "invisible" to pedestrians after a while. You know, like when you take something for granted, thinking it will always be there? After all, it had been commissioned many years earlier, in 1966, by the owner of the World Trade Center, The Port Authority of New York and New Jersey. It was completed over four years later, coinciding with the opening of the towers. From that point on, it was referred to as *The Sphere*.

With fresh, naïve eyes, *The Sphere* left an impression in my heart as my first warm "welcome" to this big city. Little did I know that this iconic sculpture, symbolizing world peace, would later become a monument coveted by the people of New York—and the rest of us.

At the end of my conference, I took a photo of *The Sphere*. Unbeknownst to me at the time, I would revisit the sculpture many times over the years—seeing it in various conditions and locations.

Drawn Back to Mourn *The Sphere*

In 2006, I returned to New York City with my oldest daughter. While it was a trip to bond and enjoy our time together, I also insisted we visit the 9/11 site, the Museum of Jewish Heritage, and other historic, educational sites. My daughter was a political science major at university, and I wanted to ensure this trip was not only pleasurable but informative. In what other city could you absorb so much history, culture, and entertainment?

When my daughter was born, my family and friends would always comment: "She's just like you." It annoyed me at the time. She was *better* than me. She was a unique individual—and even as a child she was strong, independent, and confident. But as I write this, years later, I now see how much she is like me, and I am flattered and grateful. She loves travel and adventure and works hard to achieve the far-reaching goals she has set for herself. I feel fortunate that I was able to bring her on that trip and enjoy our activity-laden week. However, unknown to us at the time, the week was filled with events that would further connect Koenig's "biggest child" with my own.

Upon our arrival, we checked into our hotel situated in the middle of Times Square. It was noisy, crowded, and oh, so perfect. We went for dinner at a restaurant nearby and discussed our plans for the next day—visiting the site of the World Trade Center.

We got up early, had a continental breakfast in the hotel, and donned comfortable walking shoes as we embarked on the first leg of our journey. With the Twin Towers destroyed years earlier, we braced ourselves for what we were about to see. But as we approached the landmark on a cold, windy morning, it wasn't at all what we expected.

We arrived at a block of land that was barricaded with heavy-duty steel fences, and we looked down into a deep pit of dirt and activity. We gulped as we tried to absorb what we saw before us.

The property surrounding the World Trade Center was now an active construction site. Side by side, my daughter and I stood alongside many others forming a twisted line—a group of strangers standing together in mourning. The mood was heavy as I reflected on my memories of the once-vibrant plaza. We grieved silently for the victims who lost their lives here, but somehow a new energy was unveiled. It was now a flattened landscape lying deep before us—yet it was active with heavy machinery and an army of workers in hardhats bustling before us. As the graders moved dirt and engineers pointed out details on their blueprints, the grit in the dust was being felt in our hearts. The people of New York were rebuilding, recovering, restoring.

As a Canadian, years earlier, I watched the news from afar as plans to design and build a tribute for this landmark were discussed. I even met a local colleague who was chosen to help facilitate these planning sessions with visionaries, architects, and builders. Silently, and reverently, I cheered them on as their ideas and inspiration rose from the ashes.

I learned that after holding a World Trade Center Site Memorial Competition to commemorate lives lost in 9/11, design proposals were submitted from around the world. *Reflecting Absence*, designed by Michael Arad and Peter Walker, won the competition on January 6, 2004. The construction site we saw before us was the initial preparation for two large, recessed pools—precisely located on the footprints of the Twin Towers. The pools were to be surrounded by a field of trees. The deciduous, Swamp White Oak trees were to form casual rows in groves and clusters, essentially creating an abstract wall of protection around the reflecting pools.

While our hearts were heavy, the despair was quickly lifted with new hope.

On our way back to the hotel, we walked through Battery Park. I remembered strolling through this beautiful park in 1999 and wanted to share it with my daughter. It was located at the southern tip of Manhattan Island facing the New York Harbor. Boat tours were launched from here, taking visitors to The Statue of Liberty and sites along the Hudson River. My daughter and I booked this tour for the next day.

As we turned and left the ticket office, what did I see? *The Sphere*! It was battered and bruised, and stubbornly perched in a quiet, shady area. I didn't realize it had survived 9/11 and was surprised and relieved to see it miraculously standing before me. Its bronze finish was no longer glistening, and it was ripped open in spots, exposing raw metal edges and a blackened finish. Koenig's "biggest child" had survived—and now my oldest child and I were able to meet it. It was ironic to me that it was placed here in Battery Park—an area named for artillery batteries that were built to protect the region in the late 1600s. *The Sphere* now rested peacefully overlooking the harbor and pedestrian promenade. I learned Koenig himself supervised its move to this location in 2002, as well as the creation of a new base for it to rest upon.

While Koenig once called his "biggest child" a sculpture, he now called it a monument and, in his quote below, I felt the powerful sentiment of a proud parent talking about his child.

"It now has a different beauty; one I could never imagine. It has its own life—different from the one I gave to it."

– Fritz Koenig

Saying Hello Once Again

Since my first two visits, I have developed a very strong connection to this city. In 2017, I convinced my husband to visit New York City with me. It was clear that he would find the historical events of 9/11 captivating, but I underestimated the power and influence of the people we were to meet.

We booked a *9/11 Tribute Tour* with seasoned guides, who shared some riveting accounts of that day. Both guides were retired—one from the Port Authority of New York and New Jersey, and the other, as I recall, a Lieutenant of the NYC Fire Department. We felt an immediate connection with the Lieutenant. He recounted a story of being called to work September 11, 2001, but he was feeling sick. So, another senior associate took his place. Little did anyone realize what events were to transpire. The co-worker, who filled in for him, became a victim of the tragedy. Our Lieutenant friend would never recover.

Part of the reason he became a volunteer tour guide was to make sure the stories of that attack were never forgotten. He had two sons who were police officers, and both worked that day—luckily, both survived. As we walked along with the Lieutenant, he shared more personal accounts of his experience. I recall him telling us he was a former US Navy SEAL and a veteran fire fighter, yet after 9/11 he had to get grief counselling. The experience was haunting—even after several years had passed. He said many others still suffer from post-traumatic stress disorder.

Years earlier, when I had come here with my daughter, we visited the *Museum of Jewish Heritage—A Living Memorial to the Holocaust*, located in Battery Park. The words the Lieutenant used were similar to the sentiments I recalled from the museum—and it sent a shiver down my spine. Like the Holocaust, the Lieutenant didn't want people to forget what happened on 9/11. He had a personal mandate to ensure these stories were never forgotten. And like the Holocaust victims, his lifetime of memories and losses that would never heal resonated deep inside me. The parallels were profound.

The Lieutenant told us he came back to work the day after the attack for "rescue and recovery." The manner in which he referred to the victims and survivors was both raw and sensitive. When a victim was found or a body part recovered, it was respectfully covered, tenderly marked, and placed on a conveyor belt of sorts. I closed my eyes. When he described this process, I found it rather harsh, but later learned that it was an effective way to manage the carnage of the event with the highest level of compassion and efficiency. As each covered and marked finding passed the rescue and recovery team, it was everyone's cue to stop at attention and salute the recovery. There was complete silence on site—in contrast to the distant sirens and cries. The thought of this dedicated team standing at attention and saluting victims during the rescue and recovery process sent shivers up my spine and tears down my cheeks.

This emotional tour also introduced us to the Survivor Tree located on the memorial grounds. The Survivor Tree instilled a sense in me that people were desperately looking to rescue, repair, and find hope in the incomprehensible. Here, it came in the shape of a pear tree. As a survivor, this stubborn tree was not going to be burned to death. Its limbs were gnarled, broken, and charred, but it still clung to life with a few green leaves stubbornly grasped to the bough. Site workers saw it and took it upon themselves to nurse it back to health. The tree was saved, and it also seemed to save the recovery workers in a way. After nurturing it back to health, they planted it in a prominent part of the memorial ground and watched it blossom and thrive.

The inscription to the Survivor Tree is as follows:

"This Callery pear tree stands distinct from the hundreds of swamp white oak trees on the Memorial. It was discovered amidst the wreckage of the 9/11 attacks. Its bark charred from fires at the

site and many of its limbs reduced to stumps. Yet somehow, the tree, still bearing leaves, showed signs of life.

Recovery workers transported the tree to a nursery in the Bronx to be cared for by the New York City Department of Parks & Recreation. With careful tending, the stumps of burned and gnarled bark gave growth to longer and smoother branches. Replanted at the 9/11 Memorial in December 2010, this Survivor Tree burst into magnificent blossoms each spring, embodying a living symbol of resilience."

Feeling inspired and yet exhausted at the same time, my husband and I continued our tour to the now-complete *Reflecting Absence* pools—finished ten years after the attack on the World Trade Center. When I booked this tour, I was expecting a quiet, introspective memorial. But the rushing waters were deafening. The pounding pools had an unrelenting energy—possibly representing tears, despair, and unspeakable sadness.

The names of the victims were engraved atop the metre-high bronze walls that line the reflecting pools. We were encouraged to select a name, put our hand over it, and say a prayer. Many names had roses laid over them; some had miniature American flags standing erect in the engravings.

Like the deeply inscribed victims' names at the Memorial, the thundering pools of water seemed to represent a sorrow that couldn't and wouldn't be silenced.

Heading back to our hotel after this long day, we took a short cut through Liberty Park. What did we see before us? Fritz Koenig's bronze monument! It was now permanently installed in this park—overlooking the Memorial Pools forever. With a bit of research, I discovered that when the sculpture was moved here, it was led by honour guards and bagpipers, and was put into place as representatives of the Port Authority gave speeches.

The power of this sculpture kind of haunted me—yet inspired me (*and obviously others*).

While I learned the sculpture was originally designed to signify world peace and trade, it became so much more than that. It became a powerful symbol of resilience, perseverance…and hope.

This bronze, 25-ton sculpture, affectionately known as the "biggest child" of Fritz Koenig, is now home once again. And its "father" must be very proud.

CHAPTER 5

Grace in Graceland

Put on My Blue Suede Shoes as I Boarded the Bus

I have always been moved by music. It has fueled my heart and soul, stirring emotions that could energize me—make me happy or make me sad. My appreciation of music began at an early age when I begged my parents for a guitar at Christmas. That led to music lessons that eventually transitioned me from acoustic to classical guitar. Unfortunately, I soon realized that I didn't have the talent to go very far as a musician. However, it made me appreciate the dedication and creativity required to produce and perform good music.

I grew up listening to a variety of music on the radio. Country, hard rock, and bluegrass—I loved it all. String instruments, in particular, were my favourite—ranging from classical, steel, and electric guitar to the banjo, mandolin, and fiddle.

One December, I won a trip to fly anywhere in North America. *I had never really won anything, but at a local Better*

Business Bureau luncheon in the fall, I donated some canned goods to the Food Bank, and my name was drawn as the first-place winner!

For most Canadians, Maui or Palm Springs would have been an obvious choice during one of the coldest months of the year, but my husband and I decided to go to Nashville.

Having always been inspired by Paul Simon's *Graceland* album, I thought this would be a wonderful opportunity to visit Nashville, the country music capital of the world, as well as tour Elvis Presley's home, Graceland, in Memphis. We were going to Tennessee, after all, and I didn't want to miss this chance. I booked the Graceland tour online, walked into the kitchen and started singing to my husband as he was cooking dinner. *He is the main cook in our house.* "We're going to Graceland, Graceland, Memphis Tennessee." He chuckled at my silliness then quickly grabbed my hand, spun me around, and we two-stepped around the house as "Graceland" played on my phone.

My husband and I found bus tours were a great way to capture the *Reader's Digest* version of the places we visited. We always seemed to have limited vacation time and wanted to capitalize on getting the most of our holiday. After an entertaining week in Nashville, we planned a one-day trip to Memphis including Graceland and Sun Studio tours. While Lower Broadway in downtown Nashville flourishes with live country bands and honky-tonks filled with rising stars, we anticipated learning more about the roots of country music, rockabilly, and soul in Memphis. Nashville's Grand Ole Opry was steeped in history, but we wanted more.

Soon We'll be Walking in Memphis

While the highlight of our tour was Graceland and Sun Studio, it was our bus driver, Tammy, who was the backstory to the trip.

The tour to Memphis was *Tammy's* tour. She organized and managed almost every aspect of the excursion. Tammy was an outgoing woman of about forty-five years of age. Her T-shirt was adorned with large "ELVIS" text with circular lightbulb images lining the inside of each letter. This typography was then overlapped with a photo of the King in a white jumpsuit. Tammy had flushed cheeks, deep laugh lines, and a raspy southern drawl which exuded her southern charm all the more. *This was going to be an interesting trip.*

We were the second group of people to be picked up for the long day ahead. The first passenger was a nurse from Ohio, seated in the front bench adjacent to Tammy. The nurse was travelling solo, after a week-long health care conference in Nashville, and she decided this would be a stimulating way to spend a Saturday—and oh, it was.

Over the course of the next several minutes, we picked up our forty-person entourage from various hotels in Nashville. Before departing for Memphis, however, Tammy stood up and asked the group who would like to wear her special gold-framed Elvis sunglasses and bedazzled ivory cape. Whoever could do the best Elvis impersonation would have the privilege of wearing the ensemble. With a procession of want-to-be singers, a winner was finally chosen from the back of the bus, and the passenger was bestowed with the eccentric costume. Without further ado, Tammy popped an *Elvis Greatest Hits* CD into the stereo, and we were off.

Truckin' down I-40 W for about an hour, we realized the heater wasn't working on the bus and the passengers, particularly in the back, were getting very cold. *At least the contest winner had an extra cape to wear.* It was winter in Tennessee, and it was chilly. Tammy stopped the bus several times and called in to dispatch to report the problem, but to no avail. One of the Canadian passengers, a farmer from Saskatchewan, said he could smell antifreeze. Well, Tammy decided we would just bundle up and snuggle in with our fellow passengers and continue to Memphis where she would fill up the antifreeze, and the problem would be solved.

Tammy entertained us for the entire trip as she dived into the highlights of Elvis's career and his life at Graceland, and then specified the drop-off and pick-up points once there.

While we sat directly behind Tammy, there were a couple of ladies sitting behind us from New York City, whom we picked up from The Hermitage Hotel in Nashville. Their hotel was an elegant five-star landmark built in 1910, and they looked like tough, classy women whom we chatted with briefly.

We arrived in Memphis by late morning. A bartender in Nashville warned us about Memphis, as we bragged to him about going to Graceland. "Be careful. It is a gritty, dirty, crime-infested city."

Upon our arrival, I could see what he meant. More industrial-looking than I expected, Memphis was a hub of transportation modes—including FedEx, an international airport, as well as the Mississippi River which offered a bustling water port. Although Memphis was located inland, it procured shipments from all over the world, making truck and train transportation lucrative. While it was not what I imagined, the anticipation of discovering this city took my breath away—it was rich with music, history, and culture. Like the song by Marc Cohn "Walking in Memphis," I was looking forward to *"walking with my feet ten feet off of Beale."*

To our delight (*and not surprisingly*), Tammy was an encyclopedia of "all things Memphis." We were intrigued as she drove by the iconic Wonder Bread bakery on Monroe Avenue and rattled off some interesting trivia. My husband was a huge fan of Wonder Bread as a child, and his ears perked up. Unlike my stay-at-home mom, my husband's mother worked full-time in a local laundry facility. Every morning, he was sent off to school with a cheese and mortadella (*Italian lunch meat*) sandwich, made with Wonder Bread. He still loves this special sandwich combo.

Innovation was not only in Memphis's music, but many other things, like Wonder Bread. The bakery invented a unique recipe filled with vitamins and minerals, and in the 1930s, was the first sliced bread. The building itself was large and white—designed to visually illustrate their innovative processes and pure elements that went into the product. Tammy told us the Wonder Bread bakery opened in 1921 but has laid vacant since 2013. Today, a credit union inhabits the premises and is proud to be part of the unique Memphis skyline. We found this to be a fascinating side story, down this side street in Memphis. Tammy was a treasure trove of information—trivial as well as noteworthy.

Another event was also brought to the forefront of my memories as we meandered into town. Dr. Martin Luther King was assassinated in 1968 at Memphis's Lorraine Motel after his famous speech "I've Been to the Mountaintop"—making the motel a National Civil Rights Museum. As a little girl, I remember hearing about his murder on the radio, the same radio where I listened to the soulful music of Elvis and B.B. King. Many years later, it was almost surreal to be in this city, remembering the social unrest at the time and sadly wondering how far we had come since then.

Yet, it was the music that stirred my soul the most. Memphis is the birthplace of blues music. It has been said that after working in the scorching, dusty cotton fields all week, the workers would venture down to Beale Street on the weekend searching for good music—and bringing chanting songs called "field hollers" with them. Some of the first rhythm and blues notes were developed in the music clubs lining Beale Street from these artists. My mom, who often sang as she worked in the kitchen, talked about these workers singing in the fields to help them get through a grueling day under the hot sun. Years later, I came to appreciate that this therapeutic music was not only entertaining, but it also broke through political, social, and economic barriers. More songs in history have been written about Memphis than any other city in the world.

We entered Memphis through Union Avenue. True to Paul Simon's poetic lyrics we saw a magnificent body of water before us: *"The Mississippi Delta was shining like a national guitar."*

Like all large centres (*including my own hometown*), some of the streets were a bit seedy, but the Graceland Mansion stood out with its sheer elegance—on top of a hill surrounded by oak trees.

Graceland is one of the major employers in Memphis and reminded me of a bustling Disneyland of sorts—employing up to 450 part-time and full-time people.

Tammy drove us to the front entrance of the 80,000 square foot Graceland Exhibition Centre. It housed many restaurants, gift shops, and museums as well as private planes of the Presley estate. It is the second-most-visited home in America, with over 650,000 people visiting Graceland a year—second only to the White House. Apparently, the King ranks right up there with American presidents.

Ironically, the Graceland Mansion itself was less than a quarter of the size of the exhibition grounds and the plethora of gift shops it housed. With eight bedrooms, five bathrooms, five sets of stairs—twenty-three rooms in total, the mansion was dwarfed next to the museums, shops, and restaurants.

As we exited the bus, I inhaled some crisp, December air and saw the inviting entrance to the exhibition center. I was immediately refreshed. After all, "We were going to Graceland, Graceland, Memphis Tennessee."

Echoing her microphone instructions, Tammy once again reminded everyone as to where and when she would pick us up as we exited the bus. Following a very strict schedule, Graceland's visit was going to be followed by a trip to Sun Studio. I wasn't too excited about Sun Studio at the time, until I realized the depth of artists that had catapulted their careers from within its walls. For now, I was content to visit Elvis's home while Tammy squealed out of the parking lot. She was racing to the nearest automotive shop to purchase some badly needed antifreeze.

The Graceland Mansion was a good place to visit in December. Staff said there were usually long line-ups and frustrating wait times. But today was chilly and too close to Christmas for many tourists to come. My husband and I hopped on the first shuttle bus from the exhibition center to the mansion and were each geared up with a tablet and headset for a self-guided tour. We were told Pricilla and Lisa Marie recorded stories on the tablet so we could listen to their memories as we moved from room to room. Upon our arrival, we were swiftly chauffeured to the side entrance of the mansion and proceeded down the sidewalk to the front of the house. It was small. Not a mansion at all by today's standards. In fact, many regular people in our generation had homes bigger than this. It paled in comparison to what I was expecting from "The King" but as I proceeded through his home, an intimate tour was about to begin.

While Elvis was more of my mother's era, my siblings and I were raised listening to his music on the radio. As I grew up, Elvis soared. He had many musical influences ranging from the gospel songs he heard in church, to the R&B radiating from Beale Street. His style changed and matured from his hillbilly rock beginnings to pop—ultimately returning to his soulful gospel roots.

While Elvis's music was focused, thoughtfully composed, and masterfully performed, his home lacked, shall I say, a cohesive flow as you walked from one room to the next. Each area was interesting in its own right, but they were discombobulated and disconnected from each other. I suspected that perhaps this sadly represented his life.

Touring Elvis's home, decked out with Christmas decorations from top to bottom, was a bit heartbreaking as I thought about all the family gatherings they must have had there. The front staircase was the focal point as you entered the home. It was clad in plush white carpet and took my breath away. Photos of Elvis lined the wall up the stairs. Each white-covered step was paired with a contrasting red poinsettia flanking the wall. My eyes were drawn up to the second floor, which still housed Lisa Marie's private quarters. Thick, red velvet curtains blocked the view at the top floor, cleverly concealing this vantage point.

We were then directed to the right by our tablets and looked straight into the living room where the plush white carpet continued, complete with a white, artificial Christmas tree, long white couch, and stained-glass panels of peacocks, which opened to another sitting area.

These massive, colourful peacocks dominated the room and were impressive in size and position. Much like Elvis himself, the room was larger than life in its lavish artwork. The room also contained a grand piano and what looked like a 1957 RCA colour television set. This was the most formal of all the rooms and the most pristine.

Elvis's mansion also reflected a life rich with family. Listening to Lisa Marie and Pricilla on my tablet, recounting their loving memories of Elvis, gave me a more intimate view of his life. Pictures of Pricilla and Lisa Marie filled the end tables and walls, along with photos of his parents.

His strong relationship with his mother, Gladys was very obvious. I later learned his first self-made $4 recording at Sun Studio in 1953 was for his mother titled "My Happiness." It was so tender and sent goosebumps down my arms when I heard it being played at the studio. It was a grainy, gravelly recording but his voice was so sweet and innocent as he strummed his guitar. It was a memory I will never forget. "The King of Rock and Roll" came from very humble beginnings. This was when I truly appreciated what Graceland represented. He became a peacock strutting his stuff, but he really was just a sweet southern boy who loved his momma.

We viewed his parents' room decorated with custom-designed French poodle wallpaper and exquisite furnishing. The Jungle Room, music room, kitchen, billiard, and TV rooms were all lavish, but somewhat ridiculously decorated.

The billiard room, where Elvis loved to play competitive games of pool, was decked out in gaudy, fabric-covered walls, an intricately pleated fabric ceiling, and elaborately upholstered furniture. The loud, multicoloured fabric covered each element in the entire room—all 400 yards of it!

The TV room, situated a few feet away from the billiard room, was designed in another bold style. Three TVs hung side by side on the far wall, regularly tuned to NFL football each Sunday (*a favourite sport of Elvis*)—complete with a pull-down movie screen. A lightning bolt with "TCB" was painted on the area above the black, L-shaped couches. Up to this point, I wasn't familiar with Elvis's *TCB* creed that represented "taking care of business in a flash." With a strong colour palette of yellow and black, we experienced yet another visually exhausting area.

Each room had an energy and persona of its own—the Jungle Room being the most outrageously decorated. Elvis never referred to it as the Jungle Room, but rather "the den." It was the hub of the home where he had his breakfast, played with Lisa Marie, and entertained his entourage (*sometimes called the Memphis Mafia*).

In The Trophy Building we saw Pricilla's simple, pearl encrusted wedding dress, Elvis's elegant tuxedo, and Lisa Marie's cream-coloured bassinette stuffed with toys. This warmed my heart, and the tour instantly became even more personal. Videos played of the three of them riding horses together, and it made me appreciate the life they had built within this home.

Graceland represented a bygone era to me as far as its style, size, and décor. But what was very current was the love of his family—that lived on and was reflected within its walls.

Here Comes the Sun

Sun Studio was amazing. Although the rickety building looked like it should be condemned, the feeling within the walls was electric. To stand in the recording rooms where Elvis Presley, Johnny Cash, and Carl Perkins, to name a few, were discovered and created fresh, unique music was awe-inspiring. There was a creative energy in this old, dilapidated building, and I wondered if it was that energy that kept the walls up and the creaky second floor from collapsing on top of us.

As I held the Shure 55S microphone, sensing the DNA from the blood, sweat, and tears of these pioneers, I almost cried. *Who would have thought I would be holding an artifact in my hands from such an important time in musical history?* I could almost imagine the young, creative musicians in this room, decades ago, gripping the microphone and singing their hearts out. I took a photo of my husband as he grabbed the mic and stand, and posed in the iconic Elvis "dip" attempting to sing "Jailhouse Rock." *Although we found out afterwards that this particular song wasn't recorded here.*

I later learned it was mandated by Sam Phillips, the rock-n-roll pioneer who opened Sun Studio in 1950, that the microphone must always stay in the building. No matter who bought or sold this building, the microphone would always be part of the package, part of its legacy, part of its DNA.

Even the classy ladies from New York let their hair down a bit here. We talked with them as we shopped in the crumbling, crowded first-floor gift store. Our conversation centered around how humbled we felt standing in this decrepit, musty-smelling icon of a building.

As our tour guide explained, this was a time when rock-n-roll was in its infancy. Sam Phillips discovered a revolutionary new sound. He encouraged amateur artists to record here, resulting in the discovery of many unknown artists. Phillips also broke down racial barriers and advocated for equality. He felt *the blues* got people, from all ethnic backgrounds, to sing about the difficulties and triumphs in life—to rejoice, pray, and preach about it, somehow relieving the burden of everyday life and making it easier to cope.

Discovering a Parallel Between Sam Phillips and Paul Simon

While I was researching our trip to Tennessee and singing "Graceland" softly under my breath, I delved into the history of the song and the album. I discovered the lyrics reflected Paul Simon's road trip to Graceland after his failed marriage to Carrie Fisher. Simon made it clear: "It's not going to be a song about Elvis Presley." Although "Graceland" was just a working title for Paul Simon from the beginning, once he saw Elvis Presley's grave on the Graceland estate, he was moved to tears and the name stuck, not only for the song, but the album as well.

Music influenced our trip—but I also was discovering how social and political issues were influencing music.

Like Sam Phillips, Simon wanted to break down social barriers and work with diverse cultures to create new, innovative music, amalgamating various global styles. However, while the 1986 *Graceland* album was an adventurous and ground-breaking project recorded in Johannesburg with black musicians, there was some controversy around it. Simon successfully collaborated with various artists on songs such as "Mother and Child Reunion," inspired by Jamaican reggae, and the gospel inspired "Love Me Like a Rock." This in turn raised a few eyebrows as *Graceland* was sometimes seen as a more political than musical effort. However, lesser-known musicians appreciated that this album was giving their music worldwide exposure, and this was a good thing. While there were mixed reviews, Simon was genuine in his goal to unite great musicians together to create great music.

The Long Road Home

With the chilly drive to Memphis, the heartwarming tour of Graceland, and the inspirational visit to Sun Studio, it was an emotionally draining day. We were grateful that it appeared to be coming to an end, although we now had to prepare for the long bus ride back to Nashville—with Tammy at the helm.

She picked us up promptly at Sun Studio at the designated spot and surprised us all with a set of yellow and black guitar picks, silk-screened with the Sun Studio logo. It was thoughtful and kind.

We had a quick bite to eat on Beale Street before we headed back to Nashville. The ladies from New York (*whom we had grown to appreciate on this short trip*) invited us to a renowned barbeque restaurant that made the best racks of smoked ribs and sausages with dry-rub spices in the world. It was called *The Rendezvous*, which made the invitation all the more tantalizing. The restaurant was in a back alley, in a basement, in downtown Memphis, across from the renowned Peabody Hotel. The barbecue aroma from the kitchen lingered all the way down the street. The wait was usually long, but we arrived well before the evening rush. We were able to enjoy a meal with our recently acquired friends from New York before racing back to Tammy's rendezvous spot.

We expected the bus ride back to Nashville to be uneventful. The antifreeze was filled up (*all paid for by Tammy herself—showing us her credit card receipt to prove it*). Everyone was tired, including a worn-out-looking Tammy, so we anticipated a nice, quiet drive back. *Well, that didn't happen!* Tammy talked non-stop all the way—perhaps to keep the tour group upbeat and entertained.

However, I was tired and anxious to get back to my hotel. I kept my eye on the road signs…100 miles to Nashville, 50 miles to Nashville, 10 miles to Nashville. *Yay, we were almost "home."* While I had a soft spot for Tammy, I wanted nothing more than to say goodbye to her and hightail it off that bus.

However, my Spidey-senses were tingling. I was suddenly on high alert, fearing another disruption. And then, it happened.

A few miles outside of Nashville, more trouble showed up—a semi-truck and trailer on fire. Tall, orange flames were shooting from the trailer with its melted tires exuding black smoke. The burning vehicle was positioned parallel to the lane we were travelling in. It was dark but the flames lit up the night sky. There were no emergency vehicles in sight. This had just happened, and it was scary.

Tammy, being the collaborative leader she was, asked the passengers what we should do.

I sat quietly behind her with my white knuckles clenching the arms of my seat. I was frozen and could not speak. *Just get me home safely tonight, I thought to myself. Get me off this f'n bus!*

Piping up with her opinion, the nurse said we should stop and help. Tammy was quietly blessing herself with the sign of the cross.

"Drive fast! We need to get back to Nashville—ALIVE!" shouted our lady friends from New York. With flames bursting into the night sky from the fiery semi-truck and trailer, it was only a matter of time before the entire rig was going to blow up into smithereens—with us in its trajectory.

To my relief, Tammy listened to the ladies from New York. She drove fast by the flaming truck. So quickly that we would not catch on fire ourselves, and swiftly enough so we would avoid the road being shut down once the emergency vehicles arrived.

I eyed the burning truck as we passed, and my heart raced. Not trusting that we were really out of danger, I turned in my seat to watch the flaming embers grow smaller the farther we moved beyond the scene. *We made it!* At that moment I loved those ladies from New York even more.

In retrospect, I realized that perhaps we should have stopped at the scene to assist with the burning truck, but we saw the driver standing on the side of road with his cell phone in hand. We also heard distant sirens coming down the highway, so we felt confident he was going to be safe. Tammy, to her credit, ensured that we, her passengers, all arrived safely back to Nashville.

Takin' it Home

When I arrived back home in Canada, it took a while to absorb all the experiences I had in Tennessee.

Nashville wasn't the wild *"Calgary-Stampede-type"* holiday I was expecting. And Graceland was not the kitschy experience I had heard about from others who had gone before me. They described the "King's" Polynesian-style Jungle Room filled with plastic plants and fake fur, as outrageously crass and garish.

Maybe because I had been forewarned about this, I looked beyond it. I saw the oversized, comfy chair in the corner amongst the out-of-control green shag rug, with Elvis's guitar laid tenderly across it, and remembered Lisa Marie describing it on my tablet. Her voice reminisced about sitting in that chair with her dad—snuggling, singing songs, and just being with him. That was my takeaway from Graceland. Beyond the tacky, shrine facade was an underlying love of a father, a daughter, and a family.

I also now understood that Paul Simon's *Graceland* was not the catchy, carefree music that I thought it was. The controversial story behind it gave the album so much more depth than I could have imagined. The intent to bring various artists together regardless of race, creed, or colour, was inspirational.

Stories of workers harvesting cotton, singing in the fields, and bringing life to rhythm and blues on Beale Street, in conjunction with Dr. Martin Luther King's assassination years later, seemed somehow prophetic.

This journey was a deeply moving voyage through decades of musical history scattered with some very violent bouts of civil unrest. Music is a powerful art form—so strong in fact, that it continues to reflect social, economic, and political issues everywhere, every day.

Tony Bennett may have left his heart in San Francisco, but I definitely left mine in Memphis.

CHAPTER 6

Makin' the Dough

It Starts with Passion, Craftmanship and the Finest Ingredients

It took me many years to appreciate that our annual ravioli-making family tradition was an art form. Like sculptures, music, and graphic design, preparing great food is immersed in talent, technique, and a passion to create.

My mother-in-law had been making homemade ravioli and tomato sauce for decades—carefully preparing the foundation for our feast months in advance of Christmas Eve dinner. My husband's family and our children looked forward to this holiday meal every year. Often the homemade pasta and filling were more cherished than the turkey dinner on Christmas Day.

Every Christmas Eve, we squished around the crowded festive table anticipating the ravioli with watering mouths. Gramma lovingly placed each ravioli on a plate, counting them prudently, covering them with sauce, and finally topping the serving with a layer of finely grated parmesan cheese. She passed the plate to me (*her assistant*), and it moved from person to person until it arrived at the recipient's place setting (*usually the youngest family member*). Once everyone was served, we sat restlessly with our knife and fork positioned vertically on each side of our ravioli-laden plate. After a Catholic Latin blessing was quickly recited, the much-anticipated ravioli was about to be devoured. Wearing our comfortable stretchy pants and with our napkins tucked under our chins, so as to not stain our finest shirts with tomato sauce, we were eager for the first morsels to touch our lips. The meal was accompanied by salads, buns, sausages, and meatballs, but the pièce de resistance was the ravioli.

Immersed in joyful and wildly animated discussions around the table, the ravioli was coveted and became the glue (*so to speak*) that kept our family congregating around that Christmas Eve table for generations.

As my children grew older, I would take them to Gramma's house to learn the fine art of ravioli-making. It was definitely not for the faint of heart. The process was complex. Gramma's freshly scrubbed assistants lined up for duty. And the finest of ingredients were measured for a flawless implementation of this art form. The most important ingredient was love—but it didn't need to be measured as it was always overflowing in the family *cucina*.

The poke, a pinch, and a press.

The Poke

Making the dough was the first step to creating the magic. Contrary to most recipes, there wasn't a specific, scientific cue to ensuring the dough was ready. It was an intangible *feeling* that arose when the dough was complete. However, there was one palpable component to this recipe, and it was the *bounce-back* factor. My daughters would mix and knead and knead until Gramma's astute hand came by and inspected the dough-in-progress. "Yes, it is ready" or "No, we need to work it more," were the judge's ruling remarks.

Pasta-making kind of reminds me of parenting. Like parenting, the dough should be firm but resilient. It shouldn't be too soft or too hard. And like the Pillsbury Doughboy, when you poke it with your finger, it should spring back. Okay so that was stretching the parenting analogy a bit too far, tee hee…or should I say Hoo-Hoo!

Once the dough passed the bounce-back tests, it was enclosed in plastic wrap and refrigerated for several hours. It was then taken out to rest at room temperature for 30-60 minutes. At this stage, the dough was not supposed to spring back when poked.

As you can see, *the poke* is the critical technical test to assess the dough.

The Pinch

Preparing the filling was the next step when creating this artwork. Gramma always used fresh ricotta cheese from the local Italian market. She would gleefully order it over the phone—speaking in perfect Italian to the store owner at the other end. It was an orchestrated event as Gramma asked how fresh the cheese was, how much they had in stock, and when it would be ready for pick up. As my mother-in-law's eager assistant, I would purchase the coveted cheese days before the ravioli-making operation was to ensue. The ricotta would come in two large, clear containers with snap-on lids—similar to food from the deli counter.

In order to prepare the cheese, we had to draw out the moisture from it. Cheese cloth from the Italian market became part of the required "art supplies" to complete this culinary feat. Returning home from the market, I spread the cheesecloth over the kitchen counter, and emptied the cheese containers over the loosely woven cloth. From there, I would draw up the corners of the cloth into a knot, creating a soft ball of cheese. Then a long, wooden spoon was inserted through the knot. This newly formed ball would be suspended over a very large ceramic bowl so that each end of the wooden spoon rested on the sides of the bowl. The slinged cheese ball was then placed in the fridge. Overnight, the moisture from the cheese would drip through the cheesecloth and settle in the bottom of the bowl. In the morning, the cloudy, white drippings were discarded, and the cheese was prepared for its journey to Gramma's house.

Upon arrival, my daughters would transfer the dried ingredient from the cheese cloth into Gramma's large, flowered mixing bowl. She would appear with her secret stash of expensive saffron, stored in a small, unassuming container. She carefully pinched a small amount between her thumb and forefinger and meticulously placed the vibrantly coloured spice on top of the white ricotta cheese. We watched in awe as the saffron's vividness seeped into the snow-coloured cheese, creating a fiery swirl of red, yellow, and orange. Gramma giggled like a little girl when she did this—smitten that her secret ingredient was finally revealed—and delighted to share this surreptitious detail with her granddaughters.

As a mom, I frequently tried to squeeze in a "teaching moment" so we researched why saffron was so expensive. We found out it was because it was made from the smallest part of the saffron flower, and it took 75,000 saffron flowers to make one pound of this spice.

Gramma then put a carefully measured amount of breadcrumbs into the mixture along with eggs and pepper. No salt, however, as she was on a sodium-restricted diet.

The art supplies, secrets, and the "dance of the bowls" became culinary artistry. We weren't slapping ingredients together; we were mastering a tradition—a recipe passed down from generation to generation, each with its own little "covert ingredient." My girls loved it, and I loved watching them learn this fine art form. It was magical. Only Gramma could teach them this art, and my role was simply to help orchestrate the passing of the baton—a baton that we knew would come our way all too soon.

The Press

Once the dough was removed from the fridge and properly rested, and once the filling was methodically mixed and set aside, we were finally ready to press the dough through the pasta machine.

Gramma used an old, hand-cranked pasta maker that was bolted to a circa 1950s, marble-green laminate kitchen table. The table was passed down from her mother-in-law and was located in the spare room where it awaited its annual performance. It was oval and about five feet in length, edged in chrome trim, and supported by sturdy chrome-plated legs. It was the type of table you would find in a retro diner today. The table, in itself, was a work of art. So, in essence, we were creating art on top of art!

The ball of pasta dough was cut into sections and each piece individually pressed through the machine. It was then folded and pressed through again and again until the correct thickness and width was achieved. Gramma would make the girls hold it up to the light to test if they could see their hands through the thin pasta. If it passed the test, the delicate pasta was then placed over a metal ravioli tray (*similar to an ice cube tray but with circular divots, rather than square ones*).

Small portions of the cheese mixture were placed in each one of the ten divots, and the edges moistened with a damp pastry brush. Another length of pressed pasta was placed on top of the cheese portions to create a casing. The layered masterpiece was then pressed with a small, wooden rolling pin. Each tool used in this artistic procedure was critical to its final outcome. With expertly pressed precision, the cheese was now in its final resting place—sandwiched between two delicate layers of pasta. The grand finale was to use a pasta cutter to separate each ravioli into its own entity.

Finally, the artwork was coming to its completed state. Each individual ravioli was placed on gingerly floured cookie sheets and arranged perfectly in rows—like a well-choreographed chorus line. Little did they know they would soon be frozen and saved for their big debut on Christmas Eve—and then cloaked in bright red dresses and sprinkled with fine gold dust.

The Change

Our family was as tight and supportive as ever, but like many, our extended family changed over the years. Similar to an aging ensemble, some orchestra members were replaced, and the maestro retired. That time had come in our family, too. Gramma was tired and couldn't carry out the artistry of the ravioli-making anymore. She moved to a senior's residence that didn't allow cooking in her small kitchenette. *Gramma really missed her kitchen.* A large part of her life was gone—her culinary creations were no more. She could no longer host the much-coveted Christmas Eve dinner. It was time to mourn a little bit. And it was time to pass that damn baton.

My youngest daughter reluctantly grabbed the ravioli baton. She was bright, eager, and creative. *But could she handle the pressure?* She had big boots to fill, and we would have to make the transition as smooth as possible. In passing the baton, we transformed Gramma from first violin player to conductor. When ravioli-making rolled around, Gramma was there to teach, train, and orchestrate. Arriving from the senior's residence proudly wearing her thread-bare apron and enthusiastic smile, the baton was passed.

We would carry on this old tradition with new leaders, new ideas, and modern equipment. Our powerful, mega-watt mix masters and automated pasta makers replaced the old "art tools" and made the process less laborious, but the essence of the artistry stayed intact. So, while the tools changed and our family evolved, our creativity soared with new fillings and combinations of flavours.

Our passion, work ethic, and creativity prevailed as we worked to ensure our family's future generations would experience the art of ravioli-making at its best—incorporated with the finest ingredient—*the love from Gramma's Cucina.*

We still keep Gramma's old, hand-crank pasta maker in the pantry. It's carefully stored in a box (*like an old trophy*), where she signed her name in the corner.

CHAPTER 7

COVID-19:
The Year My Mother-in-Law Died

Designing a Eulogy—Filled with Life

Passing on the "ravioli baton" to my daughter was a sure sign Gramma was getting tired. In fact, she was getting tired of many things, including her final abode on earth—*The Old Folks Home*, or more elegantly referred to as the Retirement Residence.

In her younger days my mother-in-law, affectionately referred to as *Mamma B*, was a social butterfly—giggling and prancing from table to table at local Italian dances, making her arrival known. She was the "belle of the ball," and I watched her in awe as she joyfully brought smiles to everyone she encountered. She worked the room like a pro, but as innocent as a little girl. I don't believe she was even aware of her magnetism and appeal.

We reluctantly thought The Old Folks Home would be good for Mamma B. They had painting classes and fitness programs along with knitting clubs and bingo nights. She loved being with people, and her effervescent personality was attractive. But in this new home (*as we suspected*), she missed her little Italian kitchen and never really took to the white-clothed tables in the formal dining room off the grand lobby. She was also very apprehensive about which groups she joined. While she found comfort in the weekly Catholic masses, she noticed some of the residents were gossipy and exclusive about who could join their groups.

One day my frustrated mother-in-law said to me, "This place is just like high school."

I was surprised and disappointed to hear this, especially since she quit school in grade eight and never even attended high school. But I guess the legacy of "the mean high school girls and all its drama" was ingrained in her at some point along the way. It seemed that even in The Old Folks Home there are cliques. Although she made a few friends, she found many of the residents quite judgmental about her clothes and her jewelry. She loved to dress up each day before going down to the grand lobby for her meals.

"Why are you so dressed up today? Who are you going to meet today?" they would tease.

As time went on, Mamma B became more and more withdrawn in her new home, and her health (*not the best to begin with*) was deteriorating. I took her to the numerous doctors' appointments, clinic visits, and hospital assessments. As we attended to her serious health issues, we always enjoyed each other's company, and these outings gave us lots of time to talk. I discovered more about her childhood and her family as she was growing up in Italy in the 1930s. I learned how her father went to war, but before leaving, he moved his family to the seaside, where it was safer. She also shared how her mother made her and her eight siblings' shoes from pieces of scrap leather.

It was a special time for us, and our bond grew tighter than it already was. These moments, these accounts of a life long ago and far away, were precious nuggets of her history. She was an ordinary woman with extraordinary stories to tell. Stories of adventure, humour, and heartache—each story retold in vivid detail. I guess I knew that I would weave them into her eulogy one day.

But that day came all too soon.

The Passing of the Baton

Mamma B died on a dreary October morning (*almost the same day my mother died years earlier*). Prior to her death, we were months into the COVID-19 lockdowns, and my mother-in-law had grown depressed and isolated. Because she was very sick from pre-existing conditions, we were able to visit regularly but with heavily sanctioned screening tests. Upon entering the grand lobby of the seniors' home, our temperatures were taken, and a questionnaire completed before gaining admittance. Sometimes, it was hard to be patient with this strict protocol, particularly on the morning she died.

When we were finally allowed to enter Mamma B's room, it was dark and cold. Although there was a floor lamp illuminating the far corner of the suite, the area surrounding her was dim and lifeless. There were two chairs positioned on each side of her bed, just as we had left them the night before.

Overnight, my mother-by-marriage had passed and was now sleeping for eternity—but she still looked tired. I felt bad that I wasn't there when she died but somehow knew that was how it was going to end. The support worker greeted us with a hug and her sincere condolences. *Even with COVID-19, she didn't hesitate to embrace us tightly, and we welcomed it.* It was comforting.

Sadly, it was the only hug we would receive during such strange (*pandemic*) times.

The Final Dance

Days earlier, I searched my mother-in-law's suite for her beloved rosary. I found it in a music box decorated with gold trim and an image of the Pope. This was a Christmas gift to her, from me, many years ago. When I bought it way back then, perhaps I knew that it would be vital one day on her deathbed. I gently placed the rosary on her pillow.

That same day, the priest who had performed many of the Catholic masses at The Old Folks Home came to administer Mamma B's Last Rights. She was blessed and anointed and ready for her debut in Heaven.

Sadly, and strangely, it was kind of a relief to see my mother-in-law's lifeless body finally surrender. She had put up a brave and courageous fight for many years, with many complex ailments. Her vast, complicated list of meds compelled me to understand each one, its dose, side effects, and interactions they had with each other. I remember one of the cardiac clinic nurses saying, "Adjusting her doses is like a fine dance. We have to change things slowly and smoothly. It's important to be methodical and patient as we monitor tiny changes going forward." At times, I felt like a pharmacist, conversing with the best of them in our medical appointments. I kept a detailed diary of notes from each healthcare visit. I think it helped me cope with the realization that she was slowly dying.

As my mother-in-law's spirit left us that dire Fall morning, I sat on the chair beside her, and took her stiff, cold hand in mine. We had held hands for many days before this, and it seemed completely natural for me to hold her lifeless hand in mine one last time. I cried, kissed her colorless cheek, and said a prayer for her. It was sad yet somehow peaceful, and I was glad she was now reunited with her husband and her loving family in heaven—including my parents (*her friends*), who had been gone for a long time. My mother-by-marriage was the last of them to go, and in many ways, it was harder to say goodbye to her than my own mother.

You see, my father looked after my mother in her final days. Of course, I visited often and brought food and support, but ultimately, my dad tended to my mom as she got sicker and sicker from COPD.

But Mamma B, well… she, in many ways, became my child. I cared for her, protected her, and advocated for her daily. Her voice was very soft, and her Italian accent was still very strong, even after decades in Canada. She needed me, and I needed to be there for her.

I held her hand for a long time before the head nurse came in at the start of her shift. She had just learned about this latest resident to pass away. This young nurse and I had gotten to know each other quite well over the past year, exchanging emails and phone calls almost daily regarding my mother-in-law's health. She was kind and wise beyond her years as she stood at the foot of the bed and offered me her condolences. *This, as my husband made arrangements in the hallway with the funeral home to collect his mother's body.*

While the timing didn't seem quite right, the nurse very matter-of-factly told me, "We have a policy here. You can either have your mother-in-law exit through the loading dock at the back of the building, or she can leave through the front door."

I closed my eyes in disbelief then quickly and adamantly replied, "She will be leaving through the front door."

However, I quickly amended my response, "I would like her to leave by the front door, as long as it doesn't upset the other residents."

The nurse promptly replied, "Don't worry about that. I will take care of it." She also added, "Good choice…she came in through the front door a year ago, and she should leave through the front door."

Looking back, I understand that some families want their privacy at such a sensitive time and slipping out through the loading dock was very discreet. However, I knew there was a large dumpster by the loading dock, and my mother-in-law wasn't going to be exiting that way—*not on my watch!*

Her Going-Away Outfit

After what seemed like a very long time, the funeral home workers arrived. Two large, bald men with masks entered the suite. *This sounds like a heist, and in some ways, maybe it was.* They were husky and middle-aged and greeted us with formal sympathies. I figured this wasn't their first rodeo.

Much to my chagrin, they rolled in a gurney with a body bag laying on the top of it, made of a patchwork quilt pattern. It wasn't a patchwork quilt—just printed fabric. In my mind, I thought, *"How cliché."* The body bag looked faded and worn, and I wondered how many other women had been in there before my mother-in-law. *Somehow, I suspected this bag was only used for the grandmotherly types. It's funny the things I observed at a time that should have been reverent.*

The quilt pattern seemed out of place since my mother-in-law never quilted and wouldn't be caught dead wearing an outfit with a patchwork pattern (*ironically comical, in a weird way*). However, I didn't think I could demand a "designer body bag," and I didn't really think it mattered at this point anyway.

And to be clear, I love quilting and have been seeking out classes to learn more about this artform. I recently purchased an incredible pair of quilted images designed by a colleague. The framed pieces hang proudly in my office—providing me with daily inspiration. Perhaps that is why the patchwork pattern left such an impression with me that day.

Regardless, as the two burly men entered the room, they said we could stay in the room as they "loaded her up." *Not their exact words, but the intent was the same.* My husband quickly said, "No, we will wait in the hallway."

The nurse also left, saying she would arrange for my mother-in-law to exit through the front door. Things were now happening quickly, and I was dreading, yet embracing, leaving her room as the sun started to rise and warm light burst through the windows.

When the two fellows from the funeral home wheeled Mamma B out of her suite cocooned in the patchwork bag, we motioned for them to lead the way as we formed a small procession behind them, down the second-floor hallway. There were a few workers who stood to the side as we passed. I smiled sadly, and they bowed their heads. When we got to the elevator, the two masked men skillfully squeezed the gurney into the cramped space. I remember thinking as the elevator doors closed behind them, that they had probably done this many times before. We took the stairs (*as we always did*) and waited at the bottom, facing the elevator, for the gurney to be wheeled out. As my mother-in-law exited on four wheels, I turned to follow.

What I saw before me was shocking.

Saluto

Both sides of the grand lobby were flanked with masked workers—shoulder to shoulder, standing at attention, lined up to form a human chain all the way to the front door! From the bus driver to the receptionist, to kitchen workers, nurses, and maintenance people, Mamma B was being given an honour walk. I was overwhelmed and almost lost composure. I closed my moisture-laden eyes tightly. The squeezed tears had nowhere to go but down my cheeks. It was one of the most powerful moments of my life. My sweet, sick, despondent Mamma B had the most ceremonial exit I could ever imagine.

At times, it felt like she didn't belong in The Old Folks Home, and she was far from the lively, magnetic young woman she once was—but the Retirement Residence gave my mother-by-marriage a walk of dignity and grandeur. She was not a war hero or a celebrity. In fact, she used to work in the laundry room of a local hospital, bundling sterilized sheets and linens for the sick.

Ironically, she now mirrors many of the unsung heroes of the pandemic, fighting against the virus in hospital laundry rooms everywhere.

That day she was being given the finest of farewells. She left The Old Folks Home in the same effervescent, magnetic way that she had entered a room in her glory days.

Her story on earth has ended, but through family, her legend will live on. Like my own mother, I felt an enormous duty to design a eulogy filled with stories and memories for my dear mother-by-marriage.

Days later, as we drove to her funeral, we didn't know where to put her rosary-adorned urn. *Do we put it safely on the floor in the back seat, the trunk, where?* We quickly surmised that whenever Mamma B drove with my husband and I, we had her sit in the front passenger seat. It was easier for her to get in and out, and she could enjoy the view as we drove to the Italian store, or wherever the journey took us. I always sat in the seat directly behind her.

Today was her final journey, and it seemed fitting that she sit in the front passenger seat once again. My husband lovingly secured her with the seat belt before proceeding to the church. As we sat at a red light, a confused fellow driver glanced over at the constrained urn in the seat belt. We all giggled a little (*and I'm sure Mamma B did too*), and it lifted our heavy spirts that morning.

As I stood at the pulpit of the sparsely filled, mask-laden church, I proudly recollected her life in full technicolor. I designed and wrote her eulogy with lively words and weaved many stories of her life into a colourful quilt of sorts. Perhaps the patchwork body bag was a perfect choice after all.

CHAPTER 8

The Munster Mash

Creativity Comes in Costume Design and Merry Making

One of my favourite times of year is Halloween. It's not for the candy or the parties—it's for the costumes, hair, and makeup design! Themed dinners are also a great joy for me to organize, as I get to design outfits, menus, and table settings for different times in history. As a graphic designer, design comes in many shapes and mediums, and I'm not limited to only picas or pixels!

Trick or Treat at the Boss's House

My first job after graduating from art college was working at the head office of a large retailer. I was very green and very nervous in my new position. I worked hard in college, but this was the "real world" now, and I wanted to make an impact. This first job enabled me to design catalogues, flyers, and advertisements for a national home improvement store. I learned a lot about lumber, paint, and hardware. It was interesting, and I was trying to fit in with a very diverse creative team. Some of my colleagues were quite experienced in this sector while others saw this company as just a stopover until their dream job came along. I was enjoying the job and learning a lot.

Shortly after I started working there, my boss hosted a Halloween party at her new house. She was excited to have the creative department over to christen the place—and we did just that.

I saw this party as my chance to really make an impression with the group (*in particular, my new boss*) and show my creativity outside the world of catalogs and advertising. I decided I was going to put some energy into a couple of artistic costumes.

After a lot of research, I finally chose an iconic couple from an old TV sitcom. My husband and I were going to be the husband and wife from *The Munsters*—Herman and Lily Munster of the hit television show that ran in the mid-1960s. Herman was a gravedigger and looked similar to Frankenstein with green skin and bolts in his neck. Lily looked a bit like Elvira with a long flowing gown, white skin, and long black hair.

Off I went to the fabric store to purchase some cheap, lightweight, fabric for Lily's white dress, black lace trim for the neckline and wide ribbon to highlight the waist. From there, I went to the local department store and purchased a plastic brimmed, flat-top hat for Herman, some inexpensive bat accessories, and a long, black wig.

Herman Munster had a thin face with an extremely high forehead that culminated in a square-shaped head. To create this look, I took the flat-top plastic hat I purchased and cut off the brim. I was left with a "hat" that I could fit on my husband's head to mimic a square top. I blended the space between the hat and his forehead with face putty.

Once the joint was smooth, I painted his entire face a "monster green" colour and blended it up into the "hat"— making a seamless transition to the flat head. I extended the green paint up the black "hat" and created some "hair" by snipping some from the long black wig I had purchased for "Lily" and gluing it to the edges. A long, vertical scar down his forehead flawlessly melded the head with the rest of his face. Deep shadows were painted under his cheekbones and nose with grey makeup, and his eyelids were heavily caked with white eyeshadow. Building up the contrast on his face was indeed like creating a monster.

To complete the look from the neck up, I found some thick plastic bolts from an old children's tool set and glued them to the sides of my husband's neck with crazy glue. At this point, I was going a bit crazy! I felt like a mad scientist that day, creating my own little Frankenstein.

Herman's outfit consisted of a black T-shirt, an ill-fitting sports jacket, short, ankle-length pants, completed with bulky, oversized platform boots. Luckily, we managed to find all these pieces in my husband's closet. *Okay, did I mention my husband wasn't the best dresser when we met?* At least this part of the costume was easy to put together. Herman was ready to party!

Now, I had to "put my Lily on."

For weeks prior to the party, I sewed Lily's dress. It had a square-cut neckline, trimmed with black lace, long bat-like sleeves, and wide black ribbon that accentuated the fitted waist, accompanied by a longer piece that hung from the belt. To complement the look, I constructed a bat necklace from the accessories I purchased including black cord, a circle medallion, and small bottle of black metal paint. A front view of a bat was painted across the medallion with spread wings. It was simple and surprisingly elegant. I glued the black cord to the back of the medallion thereby creating a very bold necklace.

Lily's long black hair had a thin white streak in the front, which I mimicked with spray paint. I applied white cream to my face and contrasted it with heavy black eye makeup and crimson lipstick. This culminated in quite a horrific look. I then put on my new white, floor-length gown and topped my head with the streaked wig. To complete the look, I painted a very prominent black widow's peak at the front of my centre part. As I looked in the mirror, the character looking back at me was a dead ringer for Lily Munster. The pièce de resistance was a heavy, floor-length, black cloak lined with shiny, hot-pink satin. The lining provided a pop of colour to my very black and white ensemble, sporting a heavy-duty clasp at the neckline that revealed the dress beneath it as I walked. *I kind of felt like monster royalty.*

We were so busy getting our costumes and makeup ready, we had no time to eat that day. But off we went to the party—hoping to get some snacks there.

Our arrival was met with *"oohs and aahs"* as we entered my boss's new basement rec room. My fellow artists immediately recognized the Munsters. They surrounded us and appreciated all the details of our costumes.

As the night went on, we became the hit of the party. We talked and danced and drank. We didn't eat any snacks so as to not ruin our makeup. But we continued to laugh and drink and joke with the group. However, as the evening progressed, I could see my husband was getting inebriated, and he started scratching his top hat and face makeup. As I stood chatting with my boss from across the room, I saw him rip the "square-hat" off his head and hurl it across the room. It hit the freshly painted white wall and left a long smear of green paint as it slid down the entire height of the wall. My mouth dropped, and my white-painted face turned red as I blushed profusely. I was mortified that my husband chose this party to show off his pitching arm. I did a side glance at my boss standing next to me. *Oh, oh, what was going to happen next?*

Much to my relief, my boss was more than gracious and said, "Don't worry about it. It's only paint." So, my husband and I continued to mingle after we picked up the pieces of his "head." Somehow, we ended up talking to another couple in the laundry room. It was next to the washroom as we waited our turns for the toilet. While casually talking with them, my husband said he didn't feel well and was going to be sick. To my shock, the fellow we were conversing with nonchalantly shrugged his shoulders, lifted the lid of the washing machine, and motioned for my husband to throw up in there. My husband promptly obliged him. This chap apparently had a very creative mind as well—because he then proceeded to add laundry soap, close the lid and turn the washing machine on!

I was both horrified and mortified once again. It was Halloween, but really, I had enough terror and fright for one night. I felt it was probably a good time for us to change into ghosts and disappear—and that is just what we did.

The impression I made on my boss that night was not what I was expecting but at least I had an entertaining story to tell many years later.

I think my creativity was appreciated as I ended up working at this head office for over five years. And my brave boss still invited us to her annual Halloween parties over that time period. *But we never went as the Munsters again to any of her soirees.*

My Little Monsters

As time when on, Mr. Munster and I were soon blessed with little monsters of our own—two sweet little girls who loved Halloween just as much as their momma did.

As October approached, I hoped they would want to be princesses or mermaids, but no, they wanted to be superheroes. While I looked forward to the day of making frilly frocks with bows and tiaras and shiny jewelry, my girls wanted nunchucks and webbing.

You see, my older daughter wanted to be Michelangelo, the Party Dude from the kid's cartoon *Teenage Mutant Ninja Turtles*. My younger daughter wanted to be her hero, Spider-Man. No store-bought costumes would do for my little girls!

Off to the fabric store I went once again. I bought patterns for each costume and was shocked to see all the pieces required to make these get-ups. They were very detailed, complicated outfits—but when finished they would look very much like the genuine, true-to-life characters my girls adored.

I started these outfits months earlier so I could tailor them to my girls' bodies and accessorize them properly. Step one was to layout the fabric and cut the hundreds of pieces of fabric. From the huge stuffed head of the ninja turtle to its hands, feet, and turtle shell, I prepared the pieces.

Spider-Man's outfit had to be carefully measured and the face mask meticulously cut so vision was not an issue. The head mask had large, tear-dropped-shaped eyeholes. On Halloween night, I planned to refine the look with white face paint to create the illusion of huge eyes.

All month long, I sewed and sewed and sewed. Before long, I had two incredible costumes to show-off to my girls. They were ecstatic and jumped around, giddy in anticipation of trick or treating!

Halloween night arrived, and we dressed the girls and painted their faces to blend with the costumes. Michelangelo was quite a complex costume. The head was 18-inches in diameter and stuffed with soft, polyester filling to create a very large mass. It was lined with soft fabric and sported a wide, orange fabric eye mask that tied at the back. It was designed with a huge grin on its face made from thick, white felt. My daughter looked out of the head between the teeth, and I painted her face white to blend in with the teeth—a seamless finishing touch.

My younger daughter's Spider-Man costume was a hit too. She could spin a web any size in that get-up. Once I had sewn and fitted all the details of the design together, I completed the look with the web pattern. I took white fabric paint and designed spider webs over the entire head piece, bodice, arms, hands, and boots. It looked authentic and professionally made. These costumes were passed on to various cousins through the years, and I was proud to use my creativity to bring joy to the Halloween season.

As my husband took my two superheroes out to collect candy from the neighbourhood houses, I remember looking out the front window and seeing this tiny little person with a big, round head. It was the perfect silhouette of a Teenage Mutant Ninja Turtle—and it was my little creation. The other kids stopped, stared, and pointed excitedly at her. I couldn't have been prouder.

Note: My older daughter, true to Michelangelo's character, was also a "party dude" and wore that turtle costume for many years—even into her late teens. While the body suit didn't fit her anymore, she adapted the large head, turtle shell, and green hands and feet to personify a real life "Teenage Mutant Ninja Turtle." She was met with "oohs and aahs," and of course, giggles.

KISS and Tell

A few years ago, my husband and I were invited to yet another adult Halloween party. Once again, I got excited about creating some unique costumes. I decided to sew a costume for my husband as a tribute to the 70s band KISS. While Gene Simmons was the leader of the band, I chose co-founder, Paul Stanley—I found his KISS persona of the Starchild character very attractive. His iconic white face, black star over one eye and long hair would complement my husband. A chiselled jaw line and natural good looks made my husband a shoo-in for Paul Stanley (*sans hair*).

Once again, I stewed over a hot sewing machine and designed a costume with wide cap sleeves (*filled slightly with foam to keep them stiff*) and a vest that came to a "v" at the waist. This top was sewn from shiny, silver fabric with a bold black pattern coming through the sheen. I took a pair of tight black jeans and glued silver stars down the outside seams of both legs—down to the ankles. We recycled the heavy black boots from Herman Munster's costume. Only this time, we spray-painted them silver with white stripes on the tall platforms. A bold, silver chained belt encircled my hubby's waist coupled with heavily chained, black leather wrist bands. I painted his face pure white with a prominent black star over his right eye and fitted a long, black mullet wig on his head to complete the look. To my amazement my husband had been transformed into Paul Stanley, in the flesh!

Because I had spent weeks designing, sewing, and assembling this complex creation, I ran out of time to design my own. I was going to be a "groupie," but I was so tired by that point, I decided to pull out Mrs. Munster's costume from my closet instead. I painted my face, put on my "Lily" hair, dress, and cloak and was ready for the party. While I was "just a recycled witch" I was so proud to look at my husband and see a KISS band member standing before me. He really rocked the look.

We arrived at the community hall party, once again to "*oohs and aahs*" from the crowd. We didn't know a lot of people there—only the small group who had invited us. But people started to gather around us and were in awe of our costumes, or so I thought. Many wanted to take photos. One fellow came up to us and asked if he could take a photograph. I said "Yes, of course." As I stood proudly next to my Paul Stanley look-alike husband, the man said, "No, I don't want a picture of you. I just want a picture of your husband. He looks really cool!" As I looked at the crowd, I realized they were all waiting for a picture of *just my husband!*

How ironic. I toiled for weeks over this costume, failing to have time to create my own and he was the star of the show!

Well, I did a good job, and that was something to be proud of at least.

The rest of the night was much like the beginning, people clamoured to talk to my husband and say how impressed they were with him. "Wow, you nailed it. You look just like Stanley!" They went on and on and on.

Later in the night as we walked in the hallway to the washrooms, women continued to go gaga over my husband. Their eyes were popping out of their heads, and they were swooning over him. I was never the jealous type, but I was that night. *Where did all these groupies come from? I was surprised they didn't ask for his autograph!*

While it kind of hurt my feelings that night, I must admit Paul Stanley lit up the room that Halloween, and it was great for my husband's ego as well as my own creative ego. *My inner badass was glowing quietly.*

Art in the Dining Room

My love of design didn't stop at picas, pixels, and Halloween costumes, however. Like my mother, they were woven into the fabric of nearly every corner of our lives. My younger daughter loved to cook and wanted to host a themed party for her friends. I volunteered to help her create the ambiance with the food, costumes, and table settings. She had chosen "An Evening at Versailles" and asked me to sew her a Marie Antoinette costume. I was so excited! Finally, I could design a pretty, feminine outfit! This project was something I could really sink my teeth into. Lace, heavily patterned fabric, and ribbon were eagerly purchased from the fabric store. I found a pattern in the Halloween section of the *Butterick* book and purchased it along with the other components.

Marie Antoinette's style was from the neoclassical period and was influenced by ancient Egypt and Greece—while revolutionizing it with a French twist. I worked hard to capture this look using modern fabrics and notions.

I had the privilege of visiting the Palace of Versailles a few years earlier and was mesmerized by the Hall of Mirrors, where the Treaty of Versailles was signed in 1919—thereby ending World War I. The picture in my grade ten social studies book was so vivid in my mind as I stood in this lavish room. In real life, the mirrors were discoloured, mottled and dark, but it still took my breath away.

I also recall Marie Antoinette's birthing bed that was open to huge crowds as she went into labour. In 1778, she gave birth to her first child, a baby girl. Versailles had public births to ensure girls were not switched with boys at birth, and so the witnesses guaranteed no dead babies were replaced with live ones. It was quite an eye-opener for me. I had no idea of these royal traditions during that period of time.

Of course, I also remember the exquisite gardens at the Palace. They were aromatic with citrous and other fruits. While the visit illustrated a very elaborate lifestyle, I also was shocked to learn the king and court only bathed once a year due to lack of clean running water. We were told that is why the French have the finest perfumes. They developed them to hide the stench of body odor. I found this quite fascinating, and upon my arrival home, I proudly told my father how smart the French were to invent perfumes to mask this bathing issue. He rolled his eyes and scoffed. "No, the French were not smart to do this. The Romans invented the aqueducts and brought fresh water into their homes. That is intelligence." I couldn't argue with that. Regardless, I was still enthralled with Marie Antoinette and the Palace.

All these memories swirled in my mind as I spent many nights and weekends sewing an elaborately decorated dress with a satin skirt underlay of light blue. A top layer was made of an ornately patterned fabric. It had shades of blue and gold making it rich and opulent looking. The puffed sleeves were full to the elbow and then exploded with fine ivory lace. The lace was deep and reached the wrist with a portion pulled up to the elbow and cinched with a large blue bow. The back of the dress also sported a large blue bow to match the sleeves and front bodice. Lace lined all edges of the dress to make it succulent, rich and oh, so feminine. The lace was then paired with thick, velvet piping to give substance and weight to the overall look. Finally, we created a pannier—basically the contraption that creates "false hips." My husband helped me concoct a device made with hula hoops and wire to form an undercarriage that would make the dress appear "dome-shaped." It worked. The dress was dramatic and could probably have been seen at the Palace of Versailles.

My daughter's head was topped with a tall, pure-white wig combining a swept-up bun of curls, cinched with a feather plume in the back of the head. Her face was painted a pale shade of white, her lips tinted ruby red, and a beauty mark strategically dotted her cheek.

And next, there was the décor of our dining room.

Once again, I thought back to my Palace visit. Against all odds, the Palace of Versailles designed and completed a south-facing orangery with trees gathered from Spain, Portugal, and Italy in 1663. The grove also included lemon, oleander, palm, and pomegranate trees and was designed by the great architect Louis Le Vau. The garden was also decorated with many sculptures during the reign of King Louis XIV, who preferred the scent of citrous to flowers.

In the spirit of the citrous plant, bright, round oranges were carefully scattered down the centre of the dining room table. *Yes, I know "carefully scattered" sounds like a contradiction, but my design sense wanted it to "look" scattered—unbeknownst to the viewer that it was artistically staged. Similar to an interior design magazine where a blanket looks like it was "tossed" on the back of a chair, while in fact, it was carefully placed by a designer before the shot was taken.*

I continued to decorate the table for the feast and created height with gold candlesticks at each end of the table. They housed elegant, white tapered candles. The base of the table was covered in a heavily starched white linen tablecloth—compliments of my Granny from Ireland.

I arranged each place setting with our finest china (*from my mother*)—edged in burgundy and a thick band of gold. Gold-trimmed cutlery was placed on napkins I found at the kitchen store—adorned with a gilded *fleur-de-lys*. I then made the main centrepiece of the table with clementines as a further homage to the orange grove at Versailles. At the last minute, I grabbed a crystal, Eiffel Tower-shaped bottle of cognac I had purchased while in Paris. It was now empty (*grin*), but I placed it in the centre of the clementine-filled dish to visually elevate a tribute to the French. The mix and match of cultures made decorating the table a bit more fun, and a bit more personal. My daughter cooked a feast of soup, Cornish game hens, and rice. Dessert consisted of an elaborate tray of fresh fruits and baked goods. The completed look was deliciously elegant.

While my husband and I were away for the weekend, my daughter enjoyed this special night with her friends. We were delighted to hear that her guests came dressed in period clothes, and at the end of the night, she let them eat cake.

As the years went on, I took great pleasure in creating these costumes and events for my family. As pathetic as it sounds, when it came to costumes, I always defaulted to my "Lily" uniform. While my family members donned elaborately detailed creations, I would wear my worn-out Mrs. Munster costume. But true to form for many creatives, I worked best in the background, and my biggest strength was making others look good.

From Mouse to House

Often the Brand Journey Starts with a Mouse Click

I had a special (*meaning monumental*) birthday coming up, and my younger daughter kept grilling me about what kind of present I wanted. I said a gift card would be nice, and then I could replenish my much-needed anti-aging skin care cream.

She said, "Okay, but if you could have anything in the world, what would you ask for?"

Really? Well then…

I let my imagination run wild and finally said, "Well, I have always admired those beautiful silk designer scarves from Paris. Each design is so unique yet so "on brand" at the same time. They are chic and timeless, but way too expensive."

"Let's take a look anyway," she said.

So, for fun, we went online, just to browse—and pretended we had unlimited funds to spend on a frivolous fashion accessory. It took my daughter and I quite a while to figure out how to even pronounce this fancy French name, Hermès. We couldn't even pretend to be pretentious.

As we scanned the website, I was very impressed with its clean, simple look. The logo was traditional with classic fonts coupled with an icon of a horse-drawn carriage. *This image was a homage to its beginnings in the saddlery industry serving the aristocracy.* It was minimalist, elegant, and quietly opulent. Unlike most brands, they welcomed white space (*actually, it was off-white*) and allowed the products to be the star—not the website interface. This brand also took great pride in the traditions behind the company. While it appealed to a diversity of generations, the company didn't apologize for its long heritage. In fact, it flaunted its history, stating "Hermès, contemporary artisans since 1837." *Wow—what a bold statement.* While the models were young and fresh, they brandished tradition. Hermès made it "cool" to be steeped in centuries of history while grounded in an entrepreneurial spirit—even to this day.

The scarves section of the website was vast, and we enjoyed looking through the various collections. We could filter the search via category, material, pattern, colour, and price. It served up a variety of selections based on my query. I chose a scarf and then browsed through the photo carousel. It displayed the front and back of the scarf, how it looked on a beautiful model, and then showed the various ways one could tie or arrange the scarf around one's neck. *Who knew? It made me wonder what's with the French and its obsession with the neck?* I selected my favourite scarf and put it in my digital cart pretending that I was actually going to purchase it—*fat chance.*

However, I was impressed with the interface. It was easy to move through, and the focus was on the product and only the product. Everything else was quiet and essentially disappeared into the background. As a designer, I appreciated this, for when I was young (*and a slow learner,*

I suppose), I would put several elements into my designs to make it "better." But as time went on, I realized "simple is better," and I started taking layer after layer off my designs until I was left with "just enough." The designer of this website already knew all that, and it showed in its tasteful, less-is-more approach.

My brown-eyed daughter watched me carefully as I moved through the website. I finally closed down the browser, and we both sighed as we realized we were born into the wrong tax bracket. *Oh well. It was a pleasant experience and allowed us to dream a little bit.*

Several months later, my daughter coyly handed me a boldly wrapped gift on my birthday. It was enveloped in very garish paper with a dark teal background that was smothered in pink flamingos and white Cadillacs. *Hmm, what loud, obnoxious gag gift has she gotten me this year?*

At this point, she pulled me aside from the others at our small family gathering, which was unusual. Birthdays were typically celebrated around the dining room table, where we had cake and then opened gifts. I was a bit confused, and then my heart sank as I came to imagine what *may* be in the box. I suspected she had spent too much money, and I was feeling guilty at the extravagant gift that I assumed laid within the wrapping. *The minx. I have been had!*

My daughter was cunning and had a biting sense of humour. I figured she may have camouflaged an overpriced gift in a tacky presentation to throw me off.

I looked at her in disbelief and said, "You didn't!" And she just smiled and moved her eyes to the gift as if inviting me to open it—without saying a word. While in shock, I reluctantly pried open the tape that was positioned on each side of the box holding the brash paper in place. As it was released, the paper fell into my lap. *At this point you can imagine, I felt both guilty and spoiled.*

Once ridden of its loud casings, an orange box was revealed. It was approximately ten inches square and about one inch high. There was a deep brown trim around the top edging of the box with perfectly mitred corners. The logo was printed exactly in the middle of the box lid, also in a deep brown colour. The traditional font and iconic horse and carriage was small and unassuming. Like the Hermès website, the brand was quietly luxurious—even with the bold colours.

The box itself was made from very heavy cardboard—thick and sturdy with a subtle, pebbled, leather-like texture (*an homage to its many leather goods, I later learned*). I appreciated every moment of this experience but was still apprehensive to see what laid inside. I came to realize that every component of this brand had the end user in mind. From the simple yet sophisticated website to the richly tactile box, I felt the customer journey was exquisitely mapped out and executed to perfection.

What Lies Within

I carefully lifted the lid and was welcomed with pristine white paper that was precisely folded in half. The paper kind of mimicked the white space on the website. *Clever.* There was an opening right down the centre, inviting me to pull it back. I cautiously lifted one side of the paper. *Oddly I noted this wasn't soft tissue paper. It had substantial weight, I guess to protect the artwork beneath it.* As I lifted it a flood of colours was revealed, and it took my breath away. I proceeded to lift the other side of the paper which exposed the logo and a beautifully crafted rolled hem. Never in my life did I imagine having the opportunity to open such a beautiful package. It may sound dramatic, but I was usually pretty happy with my "off the rack" purchases at the local department store. This was next level.

With great care, I extracted this silk work of art from the box. It was a heavier silk than I anticipated. It had substance and volume—not like the fine, flowy silk I imagined in my mind. The colours were vibrant and exploded with energy. I learned later that printing on both sides of silk was extremely difficult and a technique Hermès kept secret over many generations. I was overwhelmed. It once again surprised me that its brand was "quiet" (*like many of its business practices*) but its product was bold. The contrast between the two made them both even better.

I looked at my daughter who had her head slightly tilted as she watched me with amusement and nervous anticipation. I could see that she, too, wanted to embrace this special moment.

The rich pinks, greens, golds, and purples almost jumped from the fabric. The cheetah, butterflies, and leaves were flawlessly placed throughout the design. Subtle, it was not. I would have to wear this with a black top, and plain trousers. Like its website, the focus had to be on this luscious piece of artwork—nothing more.

Initially, perhaps due to my utter lack of class, I thought that when I wore this scarf, I would make sure that the tag was showing front and centre: *100% Silk, Made in France. I say that jokingly as I am not that superficial, but more often than not the tag does end up front and centre. Blush.*

After wearing the scarf, I would tenderly take it off, fold it respectfully, open the folds of white paper in the orange box and place it lovingly inside. It would rest there for the next auspicious occasion when it would once again make its grand entrance.

The Story Behind the Orange Box

Admittedly, I was a bit surprised by the bright orange box. I expected something more austere and classic. After a bit of research, I learned that the original box was made of white or cream coloured cardboard with gold edging—that palette made sense to me. But after World War II, the box maker ran out of white stock. All that was left was orange paper. Hermès embraced the bold colour change. After all, it mirrored the warm hue and texture of its large inventory of leather items, as they originated as a manufacturer of saddlery. So, they enthusiastically incorporated this bright colour into its brand packaging. *They saw it as the* **orange revolution!** *These words reminded me of Marie Antoinette as she was instrumental in provoking unrest that led to the French Revolution, which ultimately overthrew the monarchy.*

Revolution brought change.

This made me appreciate the sheer tenacity of the Hermès brand. It took risks and embraced the changes and challenges of a world recovering from war. While it went through various renditions, by the 1960s orange had become its signature colour. So, when I thought back to its history where they described themselves as "contemporary artisans since the 1800s," I came to appreciate its modern, progressive thinking throughout the centuries.

From a simple mouse click to the opening of the delivered package, the experience was delightful. The brand developed on the website worked hard to support the user experience all the way from browsing on the Internet to opening the heavy orange lid of the box in my home. I respected the simplicity of its website interface which dovetailed seamlessly into the delivered package and the audacious contents within it.

This brand truly delivered an end-to-end experience. Delightful—and deliciously unexpected.

And oh, my daughter — what can I say? I really am spoiled and blessed.

A Final Note: From House to Mouse to Brick and Mortar

As a final note, this isn't to say that only expensive brands have developed a flawless user experience. Today, most everyday brands have recognized the need to deliver a strong end-to-end customer experience—the world of online purchasing demands it. The days of walking into a "brick and mortar" store and feeling the carpet beneath your feet, the voice of someone greeting you as you enter, the carefully chosen music playing, and the psychology behind the layout and product merchandizing within the store, have also moved online. Like the orange box, we have progressed.

A Cat's Perspective

Every Vantage Point is Unique

We have a house cat named Gooey—a beautiful pure-bred Himalayan. He is a stunning combination of cream-coloured fur, grey-tipped ears and paws, and the most incredible baby blues. But he is a pretentious snob. He is not affectionate, and he rules the roost. It is *he* who dictates when you can touch him or, heaven forbid, pick him up.

When Gooey was a kitten, we had him trained to accept a harness with a leash when going outside. As a house cat, we didn't want him roaming freely in the backyard. But once he got a taste of the great outdoors, I think he yearned to be outside more. He would longingly look out the windows at the great big world beyond.

We have French doors off our bedroom that lead to a cedar deck, hot tub, and garden. The doors have blinds sandwiched in between two panes of glass that open and close seamlessly. I usually don't open them during the week, and the room remains dark. Frequently, when I walk by the room (*as my home office is opposite the bedroom door*), I see Gooey sitting on the floor in front of the closed blinds, sometimes, for long periods of time. *What can he possibly see through the closed window blinds?*

Then it occurred to me that from his perspective he *must* be seeing something as he looks up into those closed blinds. There is likely something of the outside world that he can view between the slats—a world he presumably misses dearly. Otherwise, why would he sit there?

One day, out of curiosity, I made my way toward the closed blinds, and carefully laid down beside Gooey. I moved slowly and gently so as not to disturb my anxious cat. Of course, as soon as I laid my head on the floor, my long hair touched his fur, and he ran away. I was disappointed we couldn't share this hardwood floor moment together.

However, from the ground view, I looked up into the half-inch planks of the closed blinds. There were horizontal slivers of light filtering through each slat. While not seeing the full view of the back deck, I could catch slices of it.

There was movement from the wind as the leaves on the trees blew back and forth. The clouds drifted slowly across the blue sky, and there were signs of small wildlife running through the backyard. As I laid there, rabbits, squirrels, and even the neighbourhood cat, Nella, visited the yard. Although I only saw a sliver of this activity, my brain kind of "filled in the blanks." I knew what trees looked like, and how the fluffy clouds moved in the sky. I also knew what a rabbit, squirrel, and Nella looked like because I had seen them in **full view** many times.

But today I was only getting a small portion of the backyard. *What if I only ever saw a sliver of that view?*

This made me think about perspectives. In my art training, I learned about viewpoints right from my first sketching class in grade school. One-point perspective, two-point perspective, horizon lines, and vanishing points are all critical to creating a proper technical drawing.

Later, in art college, I learned about *atmospheric perspective* and was taught to create depth through contrast, colour, and clarity. Objects close to the viewer were clear, crisp, and more detailed than ones in the distance, which were less clear and lighter in colour. High contrast created more visual interest while flat colours were softer and, well, lacklustre. Depending on our position in the scene, we all see things differently.

Each of us, including Gooey, sees things from different vantage points. Sometimes we see the entire picture, and sometimes we only see portions. Sometimes we are close to an object or setting, and sometimes we view it from a distance. It is through our unique vantage points that we formulate our opinions, ideas, and views, whether it is a backyard scene of birds and trees, or a view of political, economic, or social issues.

This notion became really clear with all the environmental issues, anti-pipeline protests, and climate change across Canada and the globe. Also, racial friction and the COVID-19 crisis have polarized our world. We all have unique viewpoints on these important matters. From vaccines to pipelines to discrimination, our world is complex. Different vantage points make our ability to form opinions even more complex.

Some perspectives are so shockingly different between people, industries, and even cultures, that it really shook me. There were even breakdowns within the same cultures—fractured from within. I was surprised how my family and friends, whom I assumed were like-minded, had such diverse points of view. Opinions so different, in fact, that it could be the catalyst to create hurt feelings, division, and even feuds.

Typically, I observe things quietly from the sidelines. And have tried to continue to do so during this tumultuous time. I read editorials, reports, and opinions about social, political, and economic issues—and just when I think I've developed a point of view, I read something else that sways me the other way. Through this process, I strive for a balanced point of view by seeing all sides and making an educated opinion, usually erring on the side of diplomacy. *But I wonder if being diplomatic implies I stand for nothing at all. Is it possible to take the middle ground and still have an opinion?*

Drawing a parallel between my cat's vantage point and my view of serious global issues may seem far removed; however, it actually brought me clarity. My takeaway was that whether the blinds were fully opened or closed, I needed to be aware that my perspective may be slanted (*literally*). By forcing myself to be more open-minded, I strive to constantly search and question my vantage point, including the detail, contrast, and values that will help me accurately assess what appears before me. Sometimes what may seem obvious is marred by a blurry, skewed perspective. I have attempted to keep an open mind so I can listen and respect people's views from all angles.

Whether it's Gooey's view of his backyard through slats in the blinds, or a comprehensive view of the world with access to a multitude of information, it's all about perspective. Watching my little house cat that day on the floor has helped me to seek well-rounded, balanced points of view on my creative journey—and ideally helped me to become a stronger, more sensitive, well-informed designer.

As for Gooey, I now leave the blinds fully open, so he gets a fuller perspective of his kingdom. He is just a house cat after all (*but don't tell him that*).

Note: While I make a conscious effort to open the blinds for Gooey, sometimes I forget, and I'll still see him once again staring up at the closed blinds. So, I go and open them for him—and many times he runs away. This makes me think that perhaps he likes to be "incognito" from the wilderness of the backyard with its many small predators and prey. This further demonstrated to me how important it is to appreciate each other's perspectives, motives, and ways of thinking.

CHAPTER 11

Every Picture Tells a Story

A Photograph and Happenstance

It was a warm Saturday morning in the spring, and my husband and I were getting our carpets cleaned. The carpet cleaner arrived early in the day and was super friendly. He had only started this job a month before and loved the immediate results he got from cleaning carpets. He also shared with us that he had lost twenty pounds since starting. It was very physical labour, but he felt so much better with the weight loss.

He was a short, prematurely bald young man who wore a white dress shirt and black slacks—very professionally dressed to clean carpets. I immediately could tell he was a nice, decent man, who smiled easily and could converse effortlessly on a variety of topics. He stood in the middle of our living room as he set up his equipment and talked about the various jobs he had before starting with the company. He was clearly very proud of his new role.

After our friendly exchange of his history and experience on the job, he proceeded to clean the carpet in the living room. We only had carpet there, and in the bedrooms, so he quickly moved from one room to the next, leaving each room cleaner, but incredibly humid as he completed them.

The final room to be cleaned was our master bedroom. He entered the room as my husband and I anxiously waited in the kitchen. Like most Saturday mornings, we were eager to get on with our errands—picking up the girls from Kung Fu and then grocery shopping.

As we impatiently leaned against the cupboards with coffee cups in hand, looking at our wrist watches, the carpet cleaner quickly ran down the hall into the kitchen, and asked "How do you know Susan Flannagan?"

A shiver ran down my spine. "What?" I asked. I couldn't comprehend what he was asking and why he was asking it. He repeated, "How do you know Susan Flannagan?"

Stop Right There

Several years ago, my mom and dad drove to a small town in British Columbia to explore the possibility of retiring there. They had spent the weekend driving around, exploring amenities and communities. Early Sunday morning, they took one last drive around a favourite community before heading home. They loved this sleepy little town and drove slowly down the street admiring the little houses gracefully displayed beyond the narrow sidewalks. Charming wooden exteriors with neatly manicured grass and colourful flowers enhanced each home. My parents were really enjoying the view on this quiet, sunny morning drive.

Suddenly, red flashing lights and blaring sirens interrupted their peaceful morning meander. The culprit was a police car directly behind them, motioning them to pull over. The officer straightened out his uniform and placed his service cap carefully on his head as he exited his vehicle to stroll over to my father's driver-side window. He proceeded to give my dad a ticket. *The ticket was for driving too slow!*

Needless to say, my parent's affection for this town was destroyed. They were both upset as they merged onto the highway for the six-hour drive back to the city, ticket stuffed in my dad's back pocket. Still visibly shaken as we greeted them upon arriving home, my dad was hell-bent on fighting the ticket. He felt it was absolutely ridiculous and unwarranted.

The court date to dispute the ticket came quickly, and my dad, armed with the ticket clenched in his fist, embarked on a solo trip back to the scene of the crime. My mother couldn't be bothered. Even though she, too, was upset, it didn't make sense to her to waste twelve hours of driving to fight a silly traffic ticket. But my dad had strong principles, and it just wasn't right to get this ticket—it was preposterous and unjust.

Dad got more and more agitated as he drove the six hours to the courthouse. He arrived thirty minutes before his case was to be heard and sat flustered in the crowded courtroom. He wondered how many other people were challenging a ridiculous infraction.

Finally, the court usher called his name. "Patrick O'Connell, please approach the front of the courtroom."

This is the Last Thing Dad Remembered That Day

There was a young, pretty woman in the courthouse that day. She, too, was fighting a traffic ticket presented to her on a holiday weekend in this small British Columbia town. She was nervously awaiting her name to be called, but instead, she heard "Patrick O'Connell, please approach the front of the courtroom." She immediately perked up as she thought *"Wow, that is a very Irish name…somewhat like my own."*

But as this tall, handsome Irishman approached the bench, he collapsed and fell heavily to the courthouse floor. The young woman rushed to this stranger's side and identified herself to the judge as a registered nurse. She immediately began to perform CPR on my dad, using chest compressions to mimic heart beats. Her newly acquired patient was in cardiac arrest, and she needed to act quickly.

A hush fell over the courtroom as this drama ensued. By the grace of God, the nurse was there that day, and the hospital was directly across from the courthouse. An ambulance was quickly dispatched. By the time the EMS arrived, the courtroom nurse had saved my dad's life as his heart began to beat again and his breathing resumed. The medical team then skillfully transferred Dad onto a gurney and rushed him across the street to the emergency room. He was assessed and then swiftly loaded onto a STARS Air Ambulance and transported to one of the best cardiac hospitals in the country—and back to his hometown once again. This wasn't how my dad anticipated the day ending. He arrived to court by car and was whisked back home through the air, above the Rocky Mountains and through the clouds.

Dad was in ICU for many days, treated, and stabilized. He was resting comfortably as our family gathered in his hospital room for a momentous reunion. The story of the heroic nurse spread through our family, and we were beyond grateful for her efforts.

She accepted our invitation to come to the hospital so we could express our gratitude. As we gathered around Dad's hospital bed with bouquets of flowers and cards of appreciation, this beautiful woman entered the room.

She was so petite in contrast to my tall, husky father, and we were awestruck how strong she must have been to perform CPR on such a large man. As she entered the room, she shyly scanned our family, seemingly unsure of how to greet us. This hero was humble and quiet. We gently encircled her and gave her hugs and spewed words of gratefulness. Almost like a carefully choreographed dance, we then all moved back to create a path to our father's bed. My dad's large hands engulfed her as she leaned in to embrace him. He looked deeply into her eyes and thanked this young lady—literally with his whole heart. After a few moments, I interjected with a request to have them pose for a photograph. I could see and feel an unparalleled bond between them, and I wanted to capture this special moment. *How many times do you meet the person who saved your life?*

Our hero had curly, blonde hair that reached her shoulders and was gently pushed behind her ears. She was wearing a sleeveless white, eyelet dress that contrasted with the blue hospital gown my dad wore. It struck me how her small frame looked so powerful next to my dad, who was a giant of a man. They held hands and their eyes filled with tears. The room was thick with emotion and soon everyone was crying with tears of joy. This gallant nurse's cheeks were slightly flushed, and her smile revealed perfectly white teeth that matched her dress. She looked like an angel as she stood by my dad in the photo.

I tucked the photo casually into the frame of a painting of Jesus hanging in our bedroom. At the time, I remember thinking that it was kind of funny to put a snapshot of my dad and another woman here, so I also put a picture of my mom next to them as well. It felt better and more complete. But as the years went on, I walked by these photos every day without paying them any heed. It was comfortable knowing the pictures were there, but I didn't dwell on them. However, I'll never forget this heroine's Irish name. It was Susan Flannagan.

It was a name we rarely spoke of after that hospital reunion—until the carpet cleaner paid us a visit that morning. "How do you know Susan Flannagan?" was quickly turned into "How do *you* know Susan Flannagan?" I asked in disbelief.

As it turned out the carpet cleaner and Susan Flannagan were partners in a small business venture! It was no surprise he was the salesperson, as he was endearing and had the gift of gab. What a small and wonderful world that we live in. We are all connected in some way, big or small.

After our friendly banter early into the cleaning appointment, the relationship with this pleasant carpet cleaner was somehow fateful. He was meant to be in our home that day and see the photo of Susan tucked into a picture frame in our bedroom—kind of an intimate position, like a family member. Of course, upon his discovery of the photo, we openly shared our heroic story of Susan Flannagan with him. Needless to say, he was not surprised at her valiant efforts. He said, "Yeah, that sounds like something Susan would do."

Who knew a picture taken years earlier, that I walked by daily and became kind of blind to, would reignite such emotion? This event was obviously stored away in my memory and revived by a chance encounter with our carpet cleaner. And how remarkable that the picture sparked such an incredible bond between two unlikely characters. It was like the photo had a story to be told and had come full circle.

And just for the record, Dad's traffic ticket was dismissed.

CHAPTER 12

A Brand Runs Deep

It's So Much More Than a Bit of Lipstick and Gloss

Okay, so I don't really have a personal brand. Martha Stewart has a strong one, as does Oprah. *Heck, Ms. Winfrey doesn't even need a last name anymore.* But I worked hard to try and create my own personal brand, starting with my magical transformation for my ten-year high school reunion. I wanted to make a good impression—and apparently, I did—at least temporarily.

Our high school had a tradition the Friday night before each reunion. We had a basketball game with the old school team.

It was the night of the big game. Everyone was excited to get a decent seat on the bleachers and cheer on our old high school team. Everyone that is, except for me and a few of my friends.

Instead, we went to the bar.

Just to backtrack a bit, our school was known for its winning football and basketball teams. My friends and I weren't athletic, and we weren't cheerleader material either. I went to a few games back then, but it just wasn't my thing. My friends and I were the nerds. In high school, we met in the library or sat at our lockers waiting for class to begin. We were smart and studious. I won the art award every year and generally avoided the pep rallies.

So, when the invitation arrived for our ten-year reunion, I had mixed feelings about attending. The dance was on Saturday night in the old school gym, which could be fun. But I wasn't too excited about watching the basketball game the Friday night prior. I guess they made it a tradition, in order to build some nostalgia and rally the old team spirit. However, I felt overshadowed by the athletes once again.

But sitting in the bar was fun, and I got to catch up with a handful of girlfriends I had known since elementary and junior high school. We were still nerds, but now we knew how to order a paralyzer—or two.

In anticipation of the Saturday night dance, I bought an expensive new dress (*well, expensive for me*). The fabric was a luxurious taupe-coloured crepe that hung off my body flawlessly (*the fabric, not my body*). Its full skirt came just below the knee and flowed gracefully when I walked. In fact, it moved with attitude. The dress had a belt mimicking snakeskin, and it cinched my waist just right (*when I still had a waist*). The broad, padded shoulders made me look strong and accentuated my slim midriff even more. I purchased some high heels that were made of similar fake snakeskin to match the belt. A heavy, gold necklace adorned the deep V-neck bodice, with over-sized gold earrings to balance the look. My long fingernails were painted the same colour as my dress and filed to perfectly symmetrical ovals.

I spent an hour or so curling my long, thick hair, bending forward at the waist, and shaking my head from side to side to give it more volume. Then I flipped back upward and brushed it into a "Farrah Fawcett" look, using tons of hairspray to keep it in place. My make-up was carefully applied with meticulous detail, finishing the look with bright, coral lipstick. It was the eighties—while I didn't wear spandex, I did have the big hair, wide shoulder pads, long painted fingernails, and bold jewelry!

Nervous for the reunion, I imagined the 80s movie, Flashdance, *and sang my favourite badass song over and over in my head. Oh, you know the line about "dancing for my life."*

I planned to walk into that reunion dance confident, poised, and classy. Ten years had passed since graduation, and I had accomplished a lot. *The least of which I learned how to do my hair and makeup properly and choose clothes that best complemented my (stubbornly pudgy) body.*

Right after high school, I was accepted into the Alberta College of Art and Design and spent four grueling years learning about composition, design, colour, typography, illustration, photography, production, and of course, art history. Art college was very hard work, and the critiques were tough. But I graduated and received a great job offer shortly afterwards. I also got married and had our first daughter, five years after graduating from college. Going to my ten-year high school reunion was going to be a time of reckoning. I felt like I had finally "arrived." All of the goals I had longed for were coming true, and I felt proud of the woman I had finally become. I gave myself an approving glance into the mirror one last time, before heading to the reunion in my brand-new blue Camaro.

I hadn't been back to high school since graduation, and it was a bit nerve racking to walk up the steps to the front door. High school wasn't fun for me. I was painfully quiet and shy. I was overweight (*something I still struggle with*), had bad skin, and long, greasy hair that stuck flat to my scalp no matter how often I washed it. I preferred the Poster Club to the Gymnastics Club. But that night, I felt great, even though my stomach was doing backflips. I said to myself, *"You've come a long way baby!"*

As I entered the school, I was met by a welcoming committee sitting at a table with lists of the attendees. I registered and was invited to search the neatly arranged rows for my nametag. After a bit of hunting there it was. To my horror it had my old high school graduation photo positioned by my name—in all its glory.

I put it on (*slightly annoyed that I had to poke little pin holes into my new dress*), and more annoyed that I had to display this unflattering high school photo on my lapel. Nevertheless, I proceeded to the gym where the music was blaring, and my friends were waiting. My curly hair bounced playfully, and my high heels clicked with confidence on the shiny linoleum floor. As I walked to the gym door, one of the "cool boys" darted ahead of me. He looked at me teasingly, bowed, and motioned his arm as he opened the gym door for me. "After you, M'lady." He was cute, and his charming smile was mesmerizing. I thanked him and he said, "My pleasure—it's been a while!"

Wow, this had never happened to me before in school. It was so nice to get some attention and have one of the popular boys (*any boy*) notice me. I have to say I was so flattered by his attention and welcomed this innocent flirtation—even as a happily married woman. It was a nice boost to my ego.

But, of course, it was short-lived.

As we entered the gym, he leaned in to read my name tag. He looked at it, furrowed his brow, and said with shock "Wow, you're *Laura!* You've changed so much!"

Then came the clincher.

"I wouldn't have held the door open for you back then—but I will open it for you now!"

Arghhh. Did that just happen? Did he really just say that?

All the time I spent preparing for the reunion, I focused on my outward appearance. Losing weight, buying the perfect dress, accessorizing it with big hair and makeup, was apparently all that mattered to some people. The fact that I earned a degree, had a great job, was happily married, and had become a good mother to a precious baby girl was overshadowed. Mr. Doorman didn't ask me what I had been doing since graduation. *He was only shocked about how I looked way back then.* After an awkward exchange, I learned he had recently graduated from university, but that was all I could gather before he darted off to introduce himself to a group of newly arrived ladies.

I had an aha moment. The picture on my name tag still represented me. The journey over the last ten years was about more than reaching my goals—it was attaining those goals with the grit I mustered while being a chubby, shy, over-sensitive, zit-faced teenager. I was proud of that self-conscious young girl from long ago, because she helped me become the woman I am today—strong and wise. Suddenly, the image of Irene Cara singing "*Take your passion and make it happen,*" from *Flashdance* started playing in my head again.

In life, as in business, I've learned not to be distracted by the bright, shiny objects (*or long, bouncy hair*) but rather the substance within. As a designer and brand champion, this story emphasized everything I have learned about brand design. If we have solid core principles, a strong value proposition in combination with a great product, we will succeed. These elements are the foundation of the brand. The look, feel, and tone of our branding are the "polish" to what's already there.

And, oh yeah, find your own badass theme song to help you dig deeper.

CHAPTER 13

Seeing Scarlett

Colours Seem Brighter Through the Eyes of a Child

After years of waiting to become a grandma, it finally happened. My daughter and son-in-law gave birth to a beautiful baby girl in late winter. Her name is Scarlett. She has blue-eyes, dark brown hair, and an ivory complexion that glows. Upon her birth, she looked like Snow White swaddled in a soft, cream-coloured blanket. My husband and I took turns embracing her hours later in the hospital room. We both cried with joy as we held this precious gift of life—tightly wrapped in flannel and topped with a bow of thick hair.

Flashback Over Twenty Years Earlier

I have always been a working mother. With a degree in visual communication, I embraced my career as a designer and worked for many large firms over the years. But as my two daughters grew and advanced through grade school, it became important for me to be there when they got home. They were growing up so fast and becoming more and more independent. I thought this would be the perfect time for me to bring more balance to my career and family life—and work for myself.

So, I started a small design company called BluBrown Communications. It wasn't too difficult to come up with the name. My older daughter had blue eyes and my younger daughter had brown eyes. My vision was to look at the world of art and design through the eyes of a child—always asking *"why."* BluBrown also represented *"blue sky thinking with feet firmly planted on the ground."*

When I was prospecting for clients, I would tell them this story and it stuck. People could relate to it. *BluBrown* also became my mantra to always look at every design challenge through fresh eyes. *Why don't we turn this upside down? Why don't we look at this project from a different perspective? Why? Why? Why?*

My creativity was flowing, and I felt my work was getting stronger with each project.

Working for myself also allowed me to attend my daughters' sports events and extracurricular activities. Previously, I would never think of leaving my downtown office at 3:00 in the afternoon to attend a basketball game or Girl Guide event. By being my own boss, I could do whatever I chose to do. At times, this meant I would have to work later that night, but it was worth it.

I had always worked hard in the corporate world and blending family and work life made me work even harder. Having said that, it was great to be around when my kids got home from school—their stories of the day were fresh in their minds, and I was there to listen. Our little family was closer than ever, and my little company was keeping me very busy, too. I was fulfilled as a mother and a designer.

Long-term clients and interesting projects gave me stability and satisfaction. My children gave me joy and inspiration.

Needless to say, years have passed, and my daughters have grown up, earned degrees, and started successful careers of their own. In fact, they both work in the design and communication field, which amazes me. My younger daughter went to the Alberta University of the Arts (*like me*), attained a degree in visual communication (*also, like me*), and works in the same newspaper building I had once worked in. My older daughter is a senior corporate communications leader in a large company. I couldn't be prouder of them.

As their careers flourished, I, too, continued to keep very busy with my design work.

Everything Became More Intense

Scarlett was born months before the world locked down due to a global pandemic. COVID-19 had arrived, and our once vibrant world had become bleak. The skies became grey, and the world stood still for many, many months.

Once our daughter finished maternity leave and went back to work, my husband and I volunteered to provide childcare for Scarlett one day a week. In our home, we could see our new little granddaughter during the pandemic's strict lockdowns. There was a stringent directive from the government that childcare was an essential service, so this enabled us to bond with our granddaughter and support our daughter. My husband and I both squeezed our five-day work week into four days even if it meant working later hours during the week so we could spend one day with our precious Scarlett.

I never really knew my grandmothers. Granny lived far away in Ireland, and Baba lived in another province and only spoke Ukrainian. So, I wasn't close to them, literally or figuratively. I really wanted Scarlett to know her gramma. This time together enabled us to build a strong bond right from the beginning.

It was during these months that the sun started to shine again through the gloomy COVID clouds. Scarlett was a young toddler, just learning to walk and talk. As the weeks flew by, we saw a colourful personality emerging. She was clever and funny and liked to read books and do art. Her playful side surprised us as she teased Grandpa with red watermelon and ripe blueberries—putting them up to his mouth and then pulling them away as she giggled. Her sense of humour and joyful spirit invigorated us.

As spring arrived, we often took Scarlett to the park—a park we hadn't visited since our own children were little—even though it was just across the street. Scarlett loved the baby swing, the small slide, and teeter totter. She was busy figuring out the lumpy grey pea-gravel texture beneath her feet. *This was new and different!*

On these outings, we'd frequently take a break, sit on the park bench, and just listen. We'd noticed the birds singing again. *It's been a long time since grandma and grandpa sat here and listened to the birds.* We'd point to the blue sky and the green trees so Scarlett could see the beautiful flying creatures soar through the air or perch on branches. She'd mimic the black crows flying overhead and bellow "Caw, caw."

We also noticed the Red Breasted Robins, and even the odd Blue Jay. However, she probably became the most excited from the multitude of jack rabbits that hopped through our neighbourhood. Our world opened up again to the colours, sounds, and movement of life around us.

On rainy days, Scarlett and I would sit on the living room floor by the big picture window. We'd play with toys, read books, and just snuggle. When the garbage man drove into our cul-de-sac, his truck was loud. We'd run to the window and watch the big rig as he slowly moved from house to house. Scarlett was fascinated as he picked up the trash from the neighbouring homes. When he emptied the last garbage can, he drove by our window again and tooted the horn as her nose was pressed against the glass. Scarlett waved to him, and he waved back—both of them grinning widely during the exchange. When any of the neighbours walked by or a car entered our street, Scarlett would once again run to the window, wave excitedly, and shriek, *"hi, hi, hi!"* She saw joy in all the activity of her small world.

We Heard the Music Again

Many years ago, my husband bought an intricately designed musical wall clock as a Christmas gift to me, during one of our trips to Palm Springs. Walking down Palm Canyon Drive, we were drawn to a soft musical sound coming from a small plaza. The harmonious chimes offered such a contrast to the hustle and bustle of the popular strip. We let our ears guide us into this charming little shop. It was filled with music boxes, wall clocks, Murano Glass, as well as a variety of sculptures and collectables—a treasure trove of all things beautiful. Immediately, we were drawn to the clock mounted on the wall behind the shopkeeper, as it played the most amazing melodies. I fell in love with it and watched and listened to it for a long time. Little did I know my husband was conspiring with the salesperson to secretly have it delivered to our home for Christmas. I was overwhelmed when I opened this thoughtful gift.

It chimed at the top of every hour and had four spinning crystals in the pendulum. Each hour the face of the clock would open up to expose three gold gears that spun as the music played. We envisioned listening to Christmas tunes being played as we sipped wine by the fireplace during cold winter nights, and we did this—for a while.

However, after a very short time, we grew irritated with the music and shut it off. I am not sure why or how, but it became annoying and distracting. The clock still kept time, but that was all it did.

When Scarlett came over, we turned it on again to see her reaction to the music and the movement. Her eyes lit up as she watched and listened to this magical clock. To our delight, it has once again become the highlight of our day. Every sixty minutes, I pick her up and race to the clock. We sway to the music and watch in amazement as the crystals rotate and the gold gear train spins. It's funny to think we shut it off so many years earlier. She helped us hear the music again and appreciate the beauty of this gift once more.

Seeing the world through the fresh eyes (*and ears*) of a child is magical. I haven't heard the birds sing in years, and certainly have never waved to the garbage man before! And sadly, I didn't even know some of the neighbours that Scarlett waved to during her visits. But that has all changed. Life is fun and colourful and bright. Even during a challenging COVID-19 pandemic, or perhaps because of it, the little things seem so much more important.

From blue to brown to scarlet, a rainbow of colours has appeared again. Bright wax crayons are now scattered across our dining room table. Baby S and I get all mucky with the water colours, and we attempt to build things (*anything*) out of the jumbo-coloured LEGO blocks strewn on the living room floor. *LEGO blocks have always been a challenge for me, but now I am figuring it out with my granddaughter.*

Scarlett and I are now both asking *"why?"* Why is the sky blue? Why is a lemon yellow? Why is an apple red? Why do we have to colour within the lines?"

My design work has never been more colourful or creative, and my sense of purpose has never been more clear.

It's funny, because as I started to write this chapter, I thought "Oh, this is just a silly little story about how I have learned to see the world through the eyes of a child."

But when I finished it, I realized this may be the most important story of all!

CHAPTER 14

I'm Sew in Love with Barbie

Hello Dolly

Much like the chapter about my house cat, titled *A Cat's Perspective*, there is a deeper story here than meets the eye. This isn't a silly story about sewing silly dresses for a silly doll. This story is about life growing up in the sixties. The ethics and values of a modern housewife and her influence on a young daughter.

This is a powerful story about empowerment, art, and design in everyday life.

Barbie was born the same year as me. Except she was created as a nineteen-year-old, so, in reality, she was almost twenty years my senior. I guess that explains why my mom wasn't too keen about Barbie and her voluptuous figure.

I, however, loved Barbie and have been fascinated with her my entire life—and even more so now that I'm a Nana and get to watch my granddaughter play with *her* Barbie dolls.

Unfortunately, as a little girl growing up in the sixties, I wasn't allowed to have a Barbie doll because she had "boobies," and my mom thought little girls shouldn't play with "grown-up dolls." However, one Christmas, I received the next best thing—Skipper, Barbie's flat-chested kid sister. Stacie, who was also Barbie's sibling, was given to my sister. The dolls arrived in a double wardrobe case filled with beautiful, hand-sewn clothes crafted by my mother. This gift was, by far, my favorite that Christmas—actually, it was my favorite of all time because it was my introduction into Barbie's world. I still remember the feeling of opening it up, removing the plastic strip around Skipper's hair bangs, and carefully going through each outfit. My sister liked her doll, but I was completely enamored with mine. It was probably the fashion aspects that were most exciting. Baby dolls were cute, but the Barbie doll family was the epitome of fashion, sophistication, and beauty. As I matured, I learned so much more about the Barbie brand.

Mom made similar outfits for Skipper and Stacie, but she used a variety of fabrics and colours for each doll. I remember one of my favourite Skipper outfits was a gold-coloured jumper with a black blouse underneath—a simple, clean, classic style. Stacie's clothes, however, were brighter and more fun than my understated, quiet fashions. Looking back, Mom seemed to match the outfits to our very different personalities.

Years later, on another Christmas morning, I finally received a real Barbie doll. I was still quite young, but I had "developed" early and started my period before I was ten years old. I guess Mom figured I had earned my wings to own this mature doll. Wearing my first training bra, I unwrapped a box in the glorious shape of a Barbie Doll! *I was very aware of the size and shape of the Barbie box. Up to this point, I disappointingly looked for it at each gift-giving occasion.*

I also opened another package containing a Barbie doll case that was once again filled with handmade clothes by my mother. One outfit in particular is fresh in my mind. It was a finely knit, olive green party dress with silver metallic flecks in the wool. It was a fitted, knee-length, sophisticated-looking dress. My mom also knitted a "mink" stole from some long-haired yarn to compliment the outfit. I remember putting Barbie in this ensemble and dancing around the room. My imagination was bursting with images of a fancy party filled with beautiful people—and my Barbie being the fairest of them all. I still get that magical feeling when I think of that moment.

I, myself, started sewing Barbie doll clothes at about nine years old. I stood over my mom's shoulder as she sewed, and I soaked up her talent as much as I could. Mom was always sewing for the neighbourhood ladies who paid her to create stylish outfits. Various silhouettes, patterns, and fabrics were used to sew some very haute couture creations. I watched and then translated her outfits into miniature versions for my Barbie. My craftsmanship was weak, but my passion was strong. As the years went on, my sewing skills and fashion sense got better and better. But my desire to sew waned in time.

When my mom died, my dad gave me her sewing machine, which at the time, was an expensive, computerized model. It sat in my basement for decades until one fabulous Christmas my granddaughter was given a very special gift by her auntie—a Barbie doll.

This is when my passion for Barbie fashions was renewed once again.

I've become addicted to sewing for Barbie. It seems a bit insane to describe how excited I get when I look at sewing patterns, while mulling over my growing collection of small print fabrics, silk, and tulle. I would visualize different outfits in my head and meticulously plan how I would put them together.

Would I use lace? Where would I place the buttons? Would they be pearl buttons or scaled-down regular buttons? Would I line the bodice? Would it be satin or light-weight cotton? Where would Barbie wear this new outfit—to work, to a ball, to a party, or to the park?

So many questions. So many pieces to sew. My passion had been fulfilled by sewing these clothes, and I'm not sure why. But I think it's because I feel incredibly satisfied when I create these beautiful garments. Each outfit becomes fuel for the next. It is an addiction that I needed to feed. It reminds me of my childhood and the happy memories Barbie brought me.

From Christian Dior (yes, really) to denim outfits and ball gowns galore, I have become a bit obsessed with sewing. I can't go to a fabric store without buying a bag of remnants and sewing notions. Sometimes, when I can't sleep, I dream about the next outfit I will make. While some people count sheep, I count pattern pieces. As my skills improve, so does my confidence. I no longer think of myself as a basic dressmaker but rather as a fashion designer for 11.5-inch dolls. I even joined a Barbie Sewing Club, where I am inspired by many talented designers around the world. And I soon learned of the Barbie phenomenon. There are conventions, and collections, and group after group of passionate Barbie fans globally.

Over time, I've accumulated a box overflowing with outfits I've made. Recently, I started to give them to children of family and friends for birthdays and special occasions. Many of the aunts would congregate around the gift box to view the clothes as they spilled out. I'm always surprised and flattered. One auntie even picked up a couple of the dresses, and upon closer inspection, commissioned me to make twenty ballgowns and party dresses of various colours and styles. She added these to her "at home" Barbie collection—an assortment that was gathered in anticipation of little visitors who came to see her. I was thrilled to fulfill this order and grateful for her enthusiasm for my craft. This gesture made me so excited to continue on this journey. It fueled me to churn out more and more.

And I do mean churn—it is a labour of love, but also an obsession that I need to feed. Like a feverish painter, I feel the only way to get better is to keep sewing—one piece after the other. I get stronger and more confident with each seam. But the most satisfying feeling is when I see the little children study each outfit and cherish each row of lace, rhinestones, and ribbon. I witness their imaginations soar as mine once did as a child. I wonder what event they see in their minds as they envision the clothes on their Barbie. Is she going to a tennis match, an art exhibition, or a charity event? Is she going to save the world?

Mattel says that Barbie's purpose is to inspire the limitless potential in every girl. She certainly inspired me as a little girl and made me believe I could be anything I wanted to be. This clarified to me that Barbie is so much more than a doll—she (*and her brand*) advocates for diversity, inclusivity, and social change.

Many of today's Barbies have smaller boobs and bigger hips. Some have disabilities, prosthetics, and wheelchairs. Barbie represents many cultures and ethnic communities around the world—all successfully following their diverse career paths. Without a doubt, this appeals to parents who want more realistic aspirations for their children (*like my mother*)—while still inspiring them with limitless potential.

There are so many layers to Barbie, which explains why I love her so much. She is not just a one-dimensional plastic doll with thick, synthetic hair. She is a doll with depth and substance who empowers little children to be the best they can be while making the world a better place. She is probably the only doll in the world that has become an empowering and inspirational icon from generation to generation.

"We mothers stand still so our daughters can look back to see how far they have come."

~ Ruth Handler, Inventor of Barbie

CHAPTER 15

A Day at the Museum

How Great Thou Art

"Nana, this one's for kids!"

My grandchild ran excitedly toward a colourful canvas. It was composed of brightly painted squares in a large frame hanging on the museum wall.

She stood several feet away with her head slightly tilted as she seemed to appreciate the simplicity of its composition. Clean. Bold. Orderly. It commanded the attention of a four-year-old—that was good art! Stanley Whitney was the painter of this wonderful painting who mixed different colours to create various hues and tones in *Blue Meets Yellow*.

While those in academia explain great art as having order, symmetry, and definiteness, the kid just inherently liked it! Bravo Stanley!

It was the first time she had been in a museum, and I was glad I was able to introduce her to the experience.

We had been in Palm Springs for a few days, and I wanted her to appreciate the strong art presence in the community. Architecture, photography, and contemporary glass were thriving and inspirational to me as a visual person.

On a hot, sunny morning—*Could there be any other type of morning in Palm Springs?*—we ventured out to see art. I had been to this museum several times over the years and really treasured the collections within its walls—from Picasso to ancient artifacts. I also appreciated the museum's clean design, which allowed the artwork to shine. The white walls, glossy floors, and clear glass railings highlighted the artwork, as well as the architecture of the building, which I found to have clean, angular lines with a mid-century vibe. Some areas were flooded in natural light, while others relied on track lighting to showcase the artwork. An outdoor art exhibit on the lower level, near the coffee shop, enabled us to activate all our senses. I felt a connection to its roots—in an odd sort of way. As a Canadian who grew up in the cold, snow-laden prairies, how could I possibly connect to desert life? I suppose opposites attract. Throughout the winter months, the sun, the sandstorms, and the water-starved desert vegetation were very appealing to a heat-deprived Canuck. I embraced the colours, art forms, and even the mid-century screen block patterns throughout the area.

As I delved into its history, I learned the Palm Springs Art Museum was established downtown in 1938. It had moved several times in the area before finding its permanent spot in 1958, where it gained more and more importance over the years. By the 1960s, Executive Director Frederick Sleight focused on the museum being a prime cultural centre of the desert. Sleight's wife, Alice, started a docent program at the Museum. As these docents (educated guides) fostered learning about fine art and the performing arts, attendance grew. *One docent in particular, became important to me further on in this story.*

Architect E. Stewart Williams was commissioned in 1974 to design the museum as it stands today—although various new wings followed in time. It's a beautiful gallery with the San Jacinto Mountains providing a backdrop to the structure. I was excited to introduce my granddaughter to this inspiring place—inside and out. Clearly, she found inspiration in the shapes and colours within, some of which echoed her name—Scarlett. Rich tones of red represent passion, warmth, valor, strength, and happiness—truly describing my darling granddaughter.

As we moved through the museum, we eventually reached the top floor, where Scarlett saw the painting that excitedly drew her in. However, the docent in charge of the floor saw us coming and looked both agitated and visibly annoyed. He scolded me as we approached and insisted that this little girl could not touch anything, run in the area, or speak loudly. Hmmm, I was not sure how many wild and out-of-control children he'd seen disrespecting his museum, but Scarlett was not one of them. Yes, I know that I am the Nana and may be slightly inclined to think my granddaughter is perfect, but Scarlett is, in fact, a very well-behaved child who listens to her grandma.

I assured the docent that she would behave, and we'd follow all the rules he barked out to us. He was skeptical and followed us closely. After a few moments, as he heard my firm instructions to Scarlett, I saw him relax a bit from the corner of my eye, but he nonetheless continued to follow a few paces behind.

I get it. He loved this museum and wanted the art to be preserved and appreciated for all visitors. This was about respecting the artwork in all its glory.

Since he was right on my heels, I decided to turn to him and strike up a conversation. He seemed like a decent fellow, and I wanted him to gain my trust. I learned he was a native of Detroit and attended the College of Creative Studies as a young man. He had come to Palm Springs many years ago with his partner, who enjoyed the desert art community, and treasured all things creative. As I watched my granddaughter carefully move from painting to painting, I shared my similar education from the Alberta College of Art and Design many years ago as well. My love of art enabled me to have a fulfilling career in design. I wanted to expose my granddaughter to the world of art and design so she, too, would hopefully appreciate the elements I had come to love.

My new docent friend finally loosened up, and we excitedly dived into a detailed discussion of our backgrounds and how we ended up here. Ironically, his grandmother introduced him to art galleries as a child—another parallel. He went on to describe their frequent visits to the Detroit Institute of Arts Museum as a little boy. I wasn't familiar with this museum at the time, but I later learned it housed some of the largest and most noteworthy art collections in the country. In fact, the museum has been named the United States' best art museum in *USA Today 2024*.

This explained the docent's passion for the arts and his mandate to enforce the rules on this gallery floor so vehemently. Artwork was part of his history, and he wanted it preserved and treasured. In listening to his stories, it was good to find common ground with him and value our mutual appreciation of art and design—as well as our strong connections to our grandmas.

As I relayed my admiration for this museum, my new ally shared that they would soon be welcoming a new Chief Curator. Christine Vendredi was the former global director of art, culture, and heritage for Louis Vuitton. Her vision is to bring a fresh, new perspective to the community, which has always attracted those passionate about design, fashion, and entertainment. Bringing expertise from Paris, Toyoko, and the Pacific Rim made me excited to return again—hopefully with an enthusiastic Scarlett by my side.

CHAPTER 16

Designer Genes

Denim Fades but Genes Are Forever

My giddy granddaughter, Scarlett, was perched on the stool beside me as I sewed feverishly.

I, too, became giddy as memories came rushing back to me. This was so reminiscent of my childhood as I watched my mother sew. I was fascinated with Mom's technique and craftsmanship. The command of the fabric and the sewing machine made her such an artist in my mind.

As my granddaughter hovered over me, I felt more frantic than anything. I wasn't a gifted sewer like my mom, and I needed to really focus as I sewed. While Scarlett watched me, I was worried this four-year-old would lose interest after the first stitch. But she seemed fascinated as the brightly coloured fabric moved between the sewing machine needle and the presser foot.

But this isn't another story about sewing. It's about connection and perhaps transgenerational inheritance.

How did we get here? Well, let me back up a bit.

The sturdy, light pink box by my sewing machine was overflowing with Barbie doll clothes. I naturally assumed my granddaughter would like them. Upon receiving a Barbie doll a couple of Christmases ago, she played with them all the time, often with her mom, interacting together inside her massive Barbie house. Changing outfits, combing silky hair, and going up and down the elevator in this plastic doll house were commonplace. Or so I thought. But, after making a box full of very fashionable Barbie doll clothes, my granddaughter told me she didn't want them.

Up to this point, whenever she came over, I would excitedly show her the new clothes I made for her— proudly displayed on one of the many dolls I found scattered around the house. Her new reaction was a disinterested "meh."

She likes baby dolls now.

So, off we went to Walmart to buy a 5-pack fabric bundle of coordinated cotton, covered in unicorn images (pink, purple, yellow, with some sprinkled with star patterns). The designs on the fabric were just the right scale for her 16" tall baby doll.

When we got home I showed her the doll pattern and asked which view she wanted me to make. There were jackets, pants, dresses, hats, booties and shorts.

She coordinated each garment to a fabric, but that essentially meant she wanted me to sew everything on the cover of the sewing pattern! I believe she thought sewing was like pushing a button and—voila! Done. Just like that.

Not that easy, kid.

I told her, "We'll sew them all eventually, but let's just start with one for now." I showed her how to select each pattern piece. This was a good exercise for her to search for the numbered components that I required from within the envelope. I then laid the tissue paper patterns onto the fabric and pinned them down with straight pins. She said, "Wow, this is like a puzzle."

Exactly.

At this point, I was surprised that she was still interested in the process. Her curiosity didn't wane as she followed me to the sewing room with cut materials in hand.

While it was difficult to focus on actually sewing as she leaned over me on the stool, I diligently persevered. I wanted her to see how the machine worked with the fabric.

She was vibrating with excitement as I showed her how the needle moved up and down and sewed each tiny stitch down the length of the seam. She then quickly hopped down from the stool and ran to get all her baby dolls from down the hall. She brought them into the sewing room so they could watch, too.

This was evocative of me watching over my mom's shoulder so many decades before. Was there something inherently engrained from one generation to the next? Was there an interest or propensity to possess talents and interests in similar things? It made me wonder if her Great Grandma's genes were part of her creative side.

A while ago, I had dubiously read how the events in a grandparents' lives can affect our genes. Yet, it did seem a little profound and delightfully thrilling to see so many parallels between us. I was becoming increasingly convinced there was something to this theory.

I explored this further and read many articles describing the human egg as a biological masterpiece.

I reckon the "Grandma egg theory" may have some credence. It is believed that just nine weeks into gestation, the female fetus will start producing all the eggs she will carry for the rest of her life—a whopping 1-2 million of them. What is really mind-blowing is the egg that created each of us was inside our mom— when she was inside our grandma. This connects three generations: when your grandmother was carrying your mother in her uterus, you were a tiny egg in your mom's ovaries.

So, if this research is accurate, it appears we have come full circle in our designer genes. Colourful, creative threads seem to weave a tight bond between us - my mom, me, my daughter, and granddaughter. Our love of dolls, puzzles, art, fashion, and even language, are the fabric that wraps us together. Our designer genes are truly a masterpiece.

CHAPTER 17

One Red Crayon

When Unprepared, Ya Better Get Creative

Many years ago, in elementary school—probably about grade two—I sat at my desk listening to instructions from my teacher, Mrs. McLeod. It was Valentine's Day morning, and Mrs. McLeod informed us that we would be making Valentine's cards during art class that afternoon. If we didn't have our coloured crayons in our desk, we were told to bring them to school in the afternoon for this project. My box of crayons was still at home because I needed them for another project that I was working on. I was so excited. Art class was one of my favourite times (*as you may have guessed*). All kinds of colourful ideas were spinning in my head.

In those days, kids walked back and forth to school with their siblings. Typically, the moms waited at home and prepared a hearty lunch. This day was no exception. My older brother and I walked home from school at noon and were greeted with hot chicken noodle soup and fried, baloney sandwiches—again one of my favourites! This was such a good day filled with all of the best things. After we devoured our lunch, my big brother and I headed back to school for the afternoon.

We lived about half a mile from school and had to cross a major roadway escorted by the grade six school patrols. So, it was important to return to school at just the right time in order to meet the patrols at the intersection at 12:45. That gave them enough time to chaperone us through the busy intersection and back to school for classes to begin at 1:00.

We were right on schedule, but as my foot landed on the schoolyard playground, I heard the bell ring, and I immediately became frozen with anxiety. My hands got cold and clammy, and a shiver went through my brain. *What was I going to do?*

You see, I forgot my pencil crayons at home! (*Maybe this doesn't sound like a monumental problem, but it was*). My teacher was going to be very upset with me, and I was going to get into big trouble. I entered the classroom and headed to my desk sheepishly. I sat there very, very worried about how I was going to complete this Valentine's Day art project without my crayons. I liked Mrs. McLeod, and she liked me—and I didn't want to disappoint her. I also didn't want her to make a spectacle of me in front of my classmates.

Mrs. McLeod was nice and smiled easily. But she had a stern side too—a side I had seen one too many times when her smile turned to an angry outburst. She was a tall, middle-aged lady with a pointy nose and short, dark hair who reminded me of a bird searching for prey. A cowlick at the crown of her head caused some of her hair to permanently stand up on end, giving her a slightly dishevelled look. This made me wonder why she didn't spend more time trying to tame that wild piece of mane. Her body was on the thin side although she had a rounded tummy, and a derriere of ample girth. *My mom envied Mrs. McLeod's body type as Mom frequently complained of her own flat bottom and lack of curves.*

Anyway, when Mrs. McLeod bent over to help a student beside me, her bottom usually bumped me and sometimes caused my books to fall off my desk. She usually wore black high heel shoes stuffed with varicose-veined feet, supported by long, thin legs (*kind of like toothpicks stuck in a marshmallow*). Again, I noticed the varicose veins only because my mom had real bad ones that made her feet turn purple at "that time of the month." Poor Mom would complain about her sore, achy varicose veins as they swelled and protruded from her slipper-clad feet. So, I was quite mesmerized that my teacher could wear high heels all day—impressive.

Mrs. McLeod would stand at the blackboard with chalk in hand, writing out her lessons. She would use the outside of her hand to wipe away the chalk, rather than a brush, making it permanently white during the school day. I remember her long fingernails because she used them frequently to point out things on the board, leaving a wet imprint beneath it. I was always worried she would scrape her nails across the blackboard if she got mad, which kept me on edge and added to my already high anxiety.

Nevertheless, in preparation of our afternoon art class, Mrs. McLeod said, "Okay, children, get out your coloured crayons. I am going to hand out pieces of white card stock for you to start your Valentine's cards."

Before she handed out the white paper, my teacher stood in front of the class and demonstrated how to fold it in half, using her thumb and forefinger to create a sharp crease. This formed a nice "card" shape.

This folding exercise gave me time to figure out what I was going to do without my crayons. *I better do something.* Even though I wanted to cry, I searched inside my desk for anything to use for this project. I couldn't admit I didn't have my crayons! And I couldn't borrow any from a classmate. Mrs. McLeod was very strict about sharing materials with other students, so that wasn't an option. She wanted us to be responsible for our own supplies.

The inside of my desk was fairly neat at the front, but the back was kind of messy. And I was determined to find some kind of colouring instrument in there. While slumped in my desk I discreetly tried to reach to the very back using my little arms—extended with big hopes. I could feel crumpled balls of paper, a liquid glue bottle, an eraser, and bits of cardboard stuffed in there. It was a menagerie of textures. I dug and dug and dug. Then, my fingers bumped into something long and cylindrical. I quickly pulled it out through the clutter and to my relief it was a red pencil.

It wasn't a very good "colouring" crayon—not the kind you get in a Laurentian Box. *You know, the one with the mountain scene on the package. In the U.S. these were sold under the brand Paradise.* Those crayons had soft, creamy leads that glided smoothly on paper and left a rich, deep colour. The pencil crayon I found was old, with a hard core of dark red lead—and the lead was very dry. I actually think it was some kind of industrial pencil that my dad used for welding or something in his steel fabrication shop. The opposite end of the sharpened lead had a silver tip with small teeth marks in it. So, either one of my siblings or I had this clenched in our mouth at some point. I don't exactly know how this pencil got into my desk, but I was grateful I found something to design my Valentine's Day card. *I had to make it work.*

Mrs. McLeod walked up and down the rows of desks and handed out one piece of crisp, white paper to each student. *How could I "fake" my way through this project without getting caught?* I didn't have a whole set of coloured pencils lined up like the other kids. I only had *one* red crayon.

Determined to get creative, I took the white paper, folded it in half, as instructed earlier, and began planning my Valentine's card. I started to draw an ornate border of red hearts around all four edges of the card. Although the pencil was old and the lead was hard, I licked it with my tongue to soften it. The moist tip of the crayon gave me a bright red colour. With this technique, I drew the border and then continued to make more elaborate designs on the white paper. I continued to wet it with my tongue and pressed hard to achieve a dark colour in some areas of my design. In other spots, I applied less pressure to create a light shade of pink, and in some areas, I produced a gentle gradation of colour that went from dark red, to pink, to white.

Mrs. McLeod walked up and down the aisles as she always did when the students worked. She liked to supervise closely and ensure we were all following instructions, and at the same time maintain order. I could hear the click of her high heel shoes coming my way as I noodled away at my creation.

As she walked down my aisle, my hands got really sweaty. *I always had sweaty palms as a kid—as the over-sensitive creative type.* Luckily, I was one of the last desks in the row, so I had time to focus on my heart ensemble. As she approached my desk, my palms became so sweaty that it was difficult to hold the pencil. *She was going to notice I didn't have my usual array of colours.*

Then, she suddenly stopped.

Oh, oh, I have been caught—red handed!

But instead of yelling at me, Mrs. McLeod picked up my card and walked to the front of the classroom. I gulped. She held my artwork up for the class to see. She said "Laura has only used one colour—red. A perfect colour for Valentine's Day. This is a beautiful card! The intricate red hearts contrast beautifully with the white paper to create a delicate design. I encourage all of you to pop by Laura's desk and see how she used her imagination to make this very pretty artwork!"

Wow! My work was highlighted as a fine example of simplicity and elegance. Many frustrated students turned their cards over and started mimicking my colour scheme. How incredible!

Why is this story so important to me?

Because it was a lesson in creativity and making *"do"* with what you have.

It was also a lesson in using my resources (*my brain, as well as the items at hand*) to come up with solutions. I wasn't "faking" my way out of a problem; I was creating a solution. It was an early *MacGyver* moment, and it left a lasting impression on me and, surprisingly, my children. It taught us all to think "out of the (*Laurentian*) box."

Strengthening my creative thought process is something I am proud to have developed over the years and something I continue to work on every day. My problem-solving skills have evolved from creating complex designs using one colour to learning how to be a better listener, a better collaborator, and even a better negotiator. These are skills necessary to being a good designer—and a valuable asset for, well, anyone.

Who knew one red crayon could teach me so much?

CHAPTER 18

Designing in the Dirt

Getting Down and Dirty in the Garden

I paid my way through art college by working in a garden centre over many summers as well as the winter. In the summers, my work revolved around selling and maintaining the product inventory, and in the winter, selling Christmas trees became the focus. While I wouldn't say I am an expert gardener, I became quite knowledgeable about trees, flowers, shrubs, house plants, and even fertilizers. I also learned about all the chemical herbicides and insecticides that could kill a variety of weeds and insects that lived in dirt and on plants. I discovered that steer manure was a much sought after "food" for gardening enthusiasts. We'd unload semi-truckloads full of that sh*t, and it would be sold out by the end of the day. *Steer manure and "Frank's Hot Sauce" could share the same tagline.*

Working at the garden centre was a physically demanding job. My six female besties and I would regularly unload truckloads of massive peat moss bales quickly, as the truck driver impatiently watched us. Each day, I would come home covered in dirt, peat moss, and manure. Whoever thought working in a garden centre was just about watering pretty flowers was sorely mistaken. Although it was hard work, I loved it and went back several summers over my four years of art college. I was also applying what I was learning in art college to this part-time job.

While we were usually busy in the garden centre's nursery outside, we also had an indoor shop with house plants, seeds, flowerpots, and accessories. The cash register was also inside so customers had to bring their items into the shop to pay. Frequently, they would put down their purchases and browse inside the store to see what else they could pick up. I noticed the garden centre owners (*an extended group of family members*) were only around to order supplies and pick up the cash from the sales at the end of the day. *Actually, most days, we had to drop off the wad of cash at their house.* They weren't really around to interact with their customers.

But I was.

I noticed many of the products and supplies the owners ordered didn't appeal to the customers. One item in particular that I remember was a large purchase of ugly-looking, weaved baskets, lined with plastic. They looked like cowboy hats turned upside down with a wide brim. We had a large stack of them that customers surveyed but then quickly walked away, looking confused. They were stacked beside an equally large pile of woven cloths—the size of large, square placemats. Once again, customers would look at them, shake their heads, and walk away. One day, *I thought, I am going to do something creative with these items. They weren't selling, so what did I have to lose?*

I took the stack of woven cloths, cleared a wall in the house-plants area and stapled the cloth to the wall, neatly overlapping each one to create a kind of grass-cloth-like wallpaper. This resulted in a very warm, organic room with the tan weave contrasting nicely with the vibrant green plants. I then took each of the "cowboy-hat-look-a-likes" and placed a small tack between the weaved brim to secure them into the centre of each woven cloth on the wall. It looked like hats were hanging on the wall in a very structured, geometric pattern. I also took some of the "hats," placed them at the front tables of the room, and inserted house plants into them. Customers could now see how this product was intended to be used.

The patterned wall created a rich, 3-dimensional texture that drew attention to these once-forlorn articles, and the house plants now looked "dressed up" as they sat comfortably in the weaved baskets. My goal was just to add some interest to the back wall and the house plants, but I was amazed by what happened. One by one, as customers entered this part of the shop, their eyes immediately went to the weaved pots—and one by one we *sold* them all within days. This taught me the power of merchandising. Design, imagination, and a bit of ingenuity helped us sell all of the once-ugly inventory. Long-term, this also taught me to watch (*and listen*) to customers and learn how to appeal to their needs, values, and desires. As well as create clarity around various product offerings.

Toiling in the Soil, Several Decades Later

I have always loved puttering in the yard, but landscaping was always a challenge for me as I couldn't "see" how to design around grass, trees, and flowers. But one day, I had an idea to take photos of my not-so-attractive yard and bring them into my photo-editing software. It was there, on my desktop, that I really learned to toil in the soil. I moved pixels around, added images of shrubs and trees that I imagined would work in certain areas, and visually planned my yard. It worked. For some reason, viewing my yard on my monitor helped me to imagine and organize the space. While I couldn't visualize it in my head, I could see them planted on my monitor. I designed my yard and garden using this technique and found it very enjoyable, efficient, and effective.

One day, I took on an even bigger outdoor project. We live on a corner lot with an awkward side yard—small and hard to utilize to its full potential. I decided to get creative and see what I could do with this challenging space. After a lot of trial and error, I designed a multi-tiered deck, with a hot tub inset on the top level, and a small set of stairs that led to the lower level. This second level accommodated an outdoor table and chairs and was bordered with another set of stairs running the full width of the deck, leading to a grassy area. I completed the tiered cedar deck with glass railings, lattice walls, and wooden shutters to give us privacy from the neighbours. A series of flower planters were built to highlight some areas of the yard, and block out unattractive storage areas. Designing this on my computer was a creative first step to implementing my plan. It was fun, artistic, and flexible. *Moving things around on my computer was much easier than digging stuff up in the yard and moving it around in a wheelbarrow.*

Once designed and agreed to by my husband, I took detailed measurements and drew all the components out in a vector program. This enabled me to use precise mathematical commands, so all the elements were scaled to size. My husband used this as a blueprint to build each component. My girls, along with my sister, and nephew, helped us build the deck over the summer.

Finally, I figured out how to blend dirt and design with technology. Working on the computer helped me visualize and create a variety of pretty (*as well as functional*) outdoor living spaces.

Hot 'n Heavy

Having just survived an extreme summer heat wave in Alberta, it made me appreciate how creative gardening could, and should, be. With record high temperatures locally, global warming in the news daily, and with the water crisis, particularly in California, I'd become very aware of a new gardening technique—xeriscaping. This is a concept that enables all of us to design attractive outdoor spaces that require little to no water or irrigation.

With this in mind, I took note of our south facing lawn which was burnt from the scorching sun. Our water bills were getting out of hand as we tried to keep this area hydrated. But with energy costs steadily rising and climate change becoming a serious issue, it seemed unsustainable. So, once again, I designed a creative solution to our landscaping woes. I took some photos of this area and brought them onto my computer. I selected the region of our yard that we wanted to xeriscape and drew a base mimicking black mulch over the area. The black mulch would be functional to retain moisture in the soil beneath it, as well as block out weeds. It also accented the black trim on our house.

I searched the Internet to learn about local plants that would flourish in a xeriscaping environment—junipers, potentillas, prairie crocus, silver mound, and more. I sourced images of these hardy plants and placed them into my photo, digitally. The shrubs and flowering plants added strong contrast and popped off of the black mulch backdrop. I was able to move things around visually and scale the plants to size as much as possible. My spouse was thrilled with the mock-up I showed him, and we have added a new project to our summer list. *Although, it may have to wait until next year. At least we have devised a creative plan for the future. It will not only enable us to reduce water usage, but it will also fuel our dirty little minds with more artistic gardening ideas.*

Designing digitally in the dirt enabled me to visually bring my once forlorn yard to life. Standing on the grass and trying to imagine how to landscape never worked for me. While I consider myself a creative person, there were some spaces that I just couldn't see how to improve visually in my head. But photos brought onto my computer became my canvas to "paint" digitally. I used this technique to plan and design indoor spaces, too. Before we updated our kitchen, I took photos and played with them—designing white cabinets versus dark ones, white countertops versus black. Before committing to the expense of such renovations, moving pixels and designing digitally has helped to shape my world—indoors and out.

CHAPTER 19

When I Grow Up, I Want to be a Wedding Planner

A Beautiful Brand Built into Every Detail

As with many of the stories in this book which illustrate how art and design affect our daily lives, a special event sparked such creative excitement within me, that I was consumed with it for over a year and a half. You see, it was my daughter's upcoming wedding, and it made me so elated—and I had to get everything perfect. An impossible feat for anyone. But I was willing to give it a try.

This project started with an understanding of my daughter's vision for her wedding, so I could help her bring it to life. While I didn't bake the cake, design the bridal bouquets, sew her dress, or perform the actual wedding ceremony, I was very involved in every other aspect of the event.

When vendors asked her, "What is the theme of your wedding?" My daughter would laugh and respond, "The theme is, well, *Wedding!*"

It seems like along with everything else these days, weddings have gone overboard. Truth was, she just wanted a classy, elegant day with an intimate ceremony followed by good food and lots of fun.

We went through hundreds of websites looking for inspiration. She finally chose a colour palette of rich coral, with accents of cream and dark grey. It was soft and yet offered enough contrast to create depth and visual interest.

There was so much to plan and actually implement. *We are a hands-on family!* If we could make it with our own hands, we were going to do it.

With the colour palette chosen, my daughter started to look at ideas for centrepieces. We would need thirty of them for the dinner tables at the reception, including some for other areas of the hall, as well as accessories.

In many ways, I treated my daughter like a client. It was really my daughter and her fiancé's vision for the day, and I was just there to guide, advise, and eventually implement the designs. For the centrepieces, she chose a very sophisticated flower arrangement which was to be crafted entirely by hand. To be clear, that meant I had to make each flower from scratch, ideally with the help of anyone I could coerce into assisting me.

On a vacation to the family cabin, my daughter and I designed her "prototype centrepiece." We visited all the fabric shops within a 200 km radius until we found just the right set of materials. It was a trek—a journey to find the right combination of fabrics. Each individual flower was to be conceived from a variety of patterned cloth as well as solid colours—making it rich with texture and depth. But it also made it complicated and time-consuming.

To get a sense of the magnitude of this project, each flower required forty petals. Each set of petals was cut out and slightly melted over a flame to give it a "curled, rolled edge"—kind of like a peony. We had to sew all the layers of petals together in the middle to create the final shape. The middle of the flower was then accented with some melted tulle (*fine netting*), to produce even more texture. Lastly, the centre was adorned with a combination of pearls and jewels, adding just the right amount of sparkle and shine. Each individual flower was then hot glue gunned onto an eight-inch diameter foam ball.

It took seventeen of these individual flowers to cover the ball. We then stuck a wooden dowel into the base of the ball, purchased an eighteen-inch tall "Eiffel Tower Vase" from the local dollar store, and placed the dowel into the vase. Fine white sand was poured into the vase to hide the dowel sitting in the middle of it.

But wait, it still wasn't quite done. We finished it off with some "leaves" made of white tulle. The tulle was cut in strips, folded in half, and cinched in wire that was inserted into the foam ball—filling in any little gaps with soft tufts of tulle, and creating a soft edge where the ball met the vase. Voila! We had our first centrepiece. This was truly an artistic creation. It was gorgeous—graceful and traditional, with a modern twist seen in the fabrics, crystals, and pearls.

The only problem was, we had to make twenty-nine more of these suckers! Yikes. I had to put my project management hat on and figure out how we could possibly manufacture all these within a year and a half. It sounds a bit ridiculous, doesn't it? But I was determined to do it. I did the math and calculated how many metres of fabric we needed, how many crystals, pearls, and tulle would get us over the finish line. This project involved the creation of over 20,000 petals. And we also had to make extra flowers for the other elements we had planned.

Call me crazy, but I loved every moment of it. Once all the "ingredients" were gathered, I cut the petals and organized all the components. Then I called in the troops. The ladies close to us volunteered to help us complete the centrepieces. Friends, sisters, sisters-in-law, cousins, and neighbours were gathered on a Saturday morning.

We sat around the dining room table as I gave an overview of the project with each step clarified. My daughter and I had to motivate, excite, and convince the ladies that this was going to be a fun day! *Or at least I hoped it would be.* A sample of our prototype centrepiece was placed on the sideboard for all to see. It was to be their inspiration and their guiding light.

I made a large pot of coffee and placed a dish of muffins and cookies in the kitchen. At lunchtime fresh sandwiches were served with more coffee, ice water, and fruit. We had to keep the troops well fed so they would work hard for us. Flower-making was a detailed and arduous task. *Small talk buzzed in the background as their hands whirled about the different tasks, interrupted by an occasional giggle.*

I never sat down. I was circling the table ensuring everyone had ample supplies and the quality of the work was up to par. Gosh, I sound like a drill sergeant, but it was actually a pleasant and productive gathering for the first few hours.

Each worker was assigned a specific task, and we efficiently created an assembly line. We worked and worked and worked. Some cut strips of tulle, some melted the petal edges over a flame to create the "curl," some sewed, and some embellished the flower centre with tulle, pearls, and crystals using a small glue gun.

We arranged the completed flowers on cookie sheets—a gazillion cookie sheets. They were lined up in rows, waiting to be planted into their foam flower beds. My plan was to have the "pit crew" girls create as many flowers as possible that day. Then I would assemble them onto the foam balls and complete the finishing touches by myself.

On this cold winter day, the melting of fabric over a candle, the glue gun spewing its guts at record speed, and the women starting to perspire as we cracked the whip, took its toll on us all. My house started to smell like a factory.

After eight hours of the women working full-out, we barely made a dent in all the flowers required for our twenty-nine centrepieces. And I couldn't ask them to come back for another day. This wasn't the sort of project any of these ladies would have ever taken on if I hadn't asked them. These fine ladies had toiled and moiled for many hours over hot flames, smoking glue guns, and sharp needles. It was time for them to surrender their tired minds and bodies and go home.

My grateful daughter and I thanked our chain gang and away they went. Well, basically they ran out the front door and never looked back.

You are probably wondering why we made each flower. Why didn't we just purchase the flowers and glue them onto the foam balls and save ourselves at lot of time?

Well, that just wouldn't have been good enough! We needed to choose the right fabrics, so they were all properly coordinated with other aspects of the wedding that I had planned in my head. Remember, it had to be perfect, and perfect could not be found at the dollar store.

The reality was, the bride and I spent the better part of a year working diligently each evening—to get these darn centrepieces complete. As one flower ball was meticulously completed and placed in its tall vase, I set it in front of the fireplace. Before long we had five, ten, twenty, and finally thirty centrepieces complete. They were arranged in rows in front of the hearth. I took a picture of them. They looked like a gospel choir standing side by side with matching outfits—ready to sing a hymn. The hymn that came to mind was "Hallelujah."

They were perfect and they each had a name—Daisy, Aster, Poppy, Violet, Heather, Marigold, Petunia, Bee, Rose, Peony, Lily, Hyacinthe, Crystal, Mum, Zinnia, Ally, Belle, Susan, Star, Gloria, Buttercup, Candy, Jasmine, Canna, Phlox, Clematis, Coral, Lotus, Honey, and Viola. They became my newly adopted, short, plump daughters. They were sweet, and I had a foamy soft spot for each of them.

You Are Cordially Invited

Of course, a critical element of the wedding was the invitations. This project was scheduled in conjunction with the centrepiece factory to keep everything on track. The bride had a spreadsheet of every single component of the wedding. *Did I mention we are related?* The invitations had to be designed, proofed, printed, addressed, and mailed according to the *Miss Manners' Guide to Excruciatingly Correct Behavior*.

My younger daughter, an extremely talented up-and-coming artist, designed a very impressive invitation, that was enclosed within an exquisite grey pocketed sleeve. The sleeve was a heavy, linen stock that commanded attention. It was strong and masculine, much like a well-tailored suit. What laid within it was the most feminine implementation of graphic design you could imagine.

When the heavy grey pocketed folder was opened, an ivory, pearlized paper laid within it containing elegant typography, kerned and spaced to perfection. A coral bar was positioned at the top of the page with a simple logo, which was designed using the bride and groom's initials. At the points where the two initials overlapped, a small crystal was carefully glued in place to connect the two individual letters. It was visually stunning—while representing the unity and love of two people becoming one.

To the left pocket of this folder were a series of tiered, pearlized sheets. They included instructions and maps to the church and reception, accompanied with an RSVP card and envelope. Each component had a small crystal positioned under a coral bar mirroring the invitation. When you opened this substantial grey package, the pearlized, ivory paper, crystals, and soft grey calligraphy were breathtaking. The logo design and brand that was developed set the tone for many other elements of the wedding.

The invitations were a beautiful marriage of strong design coupled with soft, tactile components portraying the flawless harmony of yin and yang. Finally, the pocketed folder and its contents were placed in a perfectly sized envelope of a similar pearlized stock. Matching digital labels embellished the outside of the package, and it was ready to be handed off to our contact at the postal service. She was going to hand-process each package to ensure it arrived in pristine condition to each recipient.

I told you everything had to be perfect.

The Red and White Club

Next came the wine labels for the reception. As an Italian family, there was little doubt the wine would be flowing freely at the reception. Each table was to be furnished with a bottle of red and white wine, and the bartenders would store the rest. Servers were instructed to restock each table with fresh bottles as the wine was consumed throughout the night. Of course, we also provided a fully stocked bar, but the wine was an integral part of the traditional Italian wedding feast.

Without thinking twice, we knew the wine labels had to be branded to match the wedding. My husband and I ordered a nice array of wines and when the dozen or so cases were delivered to our home, I painstakingly soaked each bottle in warm water to remove the original labels—front and back. As I write this, I realize how insane I sound—but at the time it seemed reasonable.

We designed wine labels for both the red and white wine, differentiating each one. Following the wedding colour palette, I purchased ivory, linen-textured self-sticking labels and designed the typography to match the font and colour of the invitations. A coral bar was placed at the top of each label with the initialized logo positioned directly below it— again, carefully embellished with a small crystal uniting the two letters. The label on the back boasted a private reserve "Best served chilled at the Ballerini Wedding."

I chuckled as I listened to David Lee Murphy's song "Dust on the Bottle" while I soaked each bottle. There certainly wouldn't be any dust on these bottles, as I was sure they would be devoured at the wedding by the time dessert was served.

While I was tempted to sample a glass as I peeled the labels off, I knew it would be counterproductive to my quality control. After each bottle was scrubbed clean—a bottle of red and a bottle of white wine were laid on a towel on my dining room table—and were carefully measured with my trusty ruler to ensure the new labels were placed at exactly the same height on each bottle. Alignment and cadence were critical to the process. Every detail became poetry.

Pews, Programs, and a Plethora

At a Catholic wedding, the church ceremony was the foundation of, well, everything. And once again, it had to be perfect. I made twenty pew markers for the first ten rows from the altar—ten on each side of the aisle.

I purchased many more yards of the same tulle we used for the centrepieces to create these pew markers. Combining layers of the tulle, I made rich, full bows with long, wispy tails that became soft tendrils as they fell lightly down the height of each pew. At the centre knot of each bow, I used the extra fabric flowers we made for the centrepieces to accent each marker. They were elegant, soft, and oh so importantly, on-brand.

Months earlier I made a prototype, and my husband and I snuck it into the church for its first "pew fitting." The ends of the pews were wide, and I wanted to design a quick and easy way to fasten the pew markers to each end post quickly and easily. Because the wedding was in August—peak season—there was another wedding directly before and directly after my daughter's. So, we had little time to decorate the church before she walked down the aisle. I had to be as innovative and as efficient as possible. With prototype in hand and with stealthy movements, we measured elastic lace loops fastened to my tulle bows that could easily slip over the pews. It was simple, easy, and effective. I had one of the members of my chain gang arrive right before the ceremony to quickly install the pew markers. *Perfecto!*

As each guest arrived at the church, they were welcomed with a well-designed program. Again, printed on pearlized stock with top coral bar and initialized logos, embellished with a small crystal. An introduction of the priest, order of the mass, hymns, attendants, and procession were detailed in the programs. Flawless once again.

Just Put It Over There Please

During the reception, in anticipation that some guests may prefer to bring envelopes rather than boxed gifts, I designed a card box to contain them. Two round hat boxes—one medium sized and one large—were purchased at the local store to create a "wedding cake" box. I carefully cut a round hole into the bottom of the top box as well as the top of the bottom box, and glue-gunned them together. In the base, I cut a "trap door" with a secure flap that could be unfastened at the gift opening to release its contents.

Once the structure was built, the real fun began. I decorated the two-tier "cake" with white textured spray paint to make it look like icing. Then many yards of coral, grey, and crystalized ribbon were purchased along with some wide lace to decorate the cake. Once in position, the ribbons looked like rows of icing piped around the base of each layer.

Finally, using more of the extra fabric flowers made earlier, I cascaded them down the tiers of the cake in a soft, diagonal direction. Crystals embellished the rows and rows of ribbon to complete the delightful looking cake box. A large slot was cut at the top to invite envelopes of all shapes and sizes to enter. The slot was also trimmed with rows of crystals. When guests first walked into the reception, it looked like a real wedding cake until they got closer to sign the guest book and realized it had an actual function (*other than eating it*).

As a graphic designer (*who usually counted pixels*), this project was the "icing on the cake." Designing an array of three-dimensional pieces for this illustrious event really challenged and strengthened the breadth and depth of my creativity.

Two posters illustrating the seating arrangements flanked each side of the door as guests entered. The alphabetized list made it fun and easy for everyone to find their table. Coordinating table numbers and menus were also developed—all branded with the signature coral bar, logo, and crystalized touches. With the centrepieces and wine bottles meticulously positioned on each table and all the other elements in place, the room was truly breathtaking as we walked in.

There was also an array of other wedding collateral, from decorated candles, to small gifts for each guest which consisted of a shot glass silk-screened with the wedding logo. A mini container of booze was also included with the shot glass swept up together in a tulle bundle, tied with a coral bow and a "thanks for coming" note.

The hall was branded so strongly that when we prepared to cue up the wedding video (*you guessed it, again heavily branded*), my niece strolled over as I was taping the extension cord across the floor. She laughed and said she couldn't believe the duct tape wasn't branded with the logo and colour palette. It was a missed opportunity!

Singing HALL-elujah Once Again

We chose our large community hall because it held many memories for us and was close to home. Our daughters had taken Kung Fu there for many years and earned their brown belts there. *I'm still upset they quit before receiving their black belts, argh.* It was also the hall where we celebrated many New Year's Eve dances hosted by the Italian Club, so it was sentimental for the wedding reception to be hosted there.

Perhaps because the building had witnessed one too many sparring matches or one too many parties, it had started to look a bit tired. But we transformed the room with our decorations and accessories. So much so that it took your breath away as you walked through the doors.

We dressed the room with white table linens and chair covers. The white enclosed chairs were embellished with wide satin coral ribbons at the back of the seat. The rear of the chair was adorned with a crystal medallion where the ribbons joined. It was classy and on-brand.

I produced a large version of the logo to hang over the white-draped back drop, behind the head table. It was a huge version of the bride and groom's initials printed in their signature coral colour. Like a Las Vegas sign that lit up the night, I glued crystal-encrusted ribbon along the edges of the 3D logo. From the side you could see the depth and dimension of this icon.

The evening was festive, fun, emotional—and came to an end all too quickly. But what made it great was that the community hall was a venue where we could basically decorate as we pleased and was void of many rules—even allowing the bride to dance on the tabletops. The Golf and Country Club wouldn't have permitted that!

I Take Thee

Much like designing for a client, developing the brand for this wedding was a fun, collaborative experience. My younger daughter and I worked diligently to support the bride and groom. While we enthusiastically jumped in headfirst to develop many of the elements, it was our duty to ensure the wedding couple's wishes were met, and they were happy with every decision that was made. When it was time to implement the approved designs, we pulled in the troops to help. We depended on specialized talents so that the music, bouquets, cake, dresses, food, bartending, and everything else was attended to.

Building a brand is so much more than designing a logo. It's marrying all the components to create a feeling, and an experience. If done right, it ensures your brand stands out in a memorable way.

After the wedding, I stored the centrepieces in large boxes in the basement closet. I wasn't sure what I was going to do with thirty custom-made centrepieces, but I wasn't ready to give them up. They were a part of my family now. I also carefully packed and stored the pew markers, tiered card cake, and decorated candles in the same closet. As time went on, I knew I would eventually have to say goodbye to them, but they were such a labour of love, I wanted to keep them close to me for a while.

It took me five years before I put an ad online to sell all the components as a package. I posted exquisitely lit photos with captions of each piece. Within a day or two, a nice lady texted me and made me an offer I couldn't refuse. When she came to pick them up, she wanted to review them to ensure they looked like the photos. She inspected the centrepieces, and picked up one of the pew markers and stroked the tulle bow. As she inspected the pieces she said, "I can see the love you put into each and every one of these creations. They are beautiful."

That was all I needed. My centrepieces and the accompanying elements had found their new home.

P.S. I kept Daisy, the original prototype design of the centrepiece. It adorns my laundry room these days, and I gaze at it frequently with fond memories.

CHAPTER 20

Finding My Inner Badass

Being Creative and Quietly Fierce

I belong to a professional networking group that meets weekly for breakfast. At the beginning of each meeting, we have a "roll call"—a sixty-second opportunity to introduce ourselves and the category we represent, share business leads for other members, and describe the challenges and successes of our week. *My company represents graphic design and branding.*

One morning, we were asked to throw our nametags into a pot. Each member had to randomly select a "new" nametag of another member and introduce themselves as that person during our roll call. I suppose it was an opportunity to see how much we had learned about fellow members in the association.

I chose the nametag of someone that I was pretty confident to introduce, and I noticed that a long-term member had selected my name. *What was he going to say about me? What kind of impact have I had in this group?* I was excited.

I've belonged to this business organization for over three years, and I joined to challenge myself. I was a naturally quiet, introverted person and I wanted to learn to be a better networker and become more skilled at expressing myself in large groups. It was working. I was gaining confidence and developing relationships in this group. I believe I am an amazing designer with a pit-bull like work ethic. *But do* **they** *see me that way?*

As the mic got passed to my "alter ego," he stood up and said "Hi, my name is Laura Ballerini. I am the nicest and the quietest member of our group. I get along with everyone, am kind, and always have a smile on my face." My heart sank. *That's it?*

I blew him a kiss. *How appropriate of me.*

Driving away from the meeting, it hit me that this wasn't the first time I'd been called "nice."

When I started my company, a colleague of my husband told me I was too nice to run my own business. He said, "You will never survive." *That was over twenty years ago!*

I left the networking event and arrived at my next meeting feeling irritated, but glad to meet with one of my long-time clients. He was a seasoned businessman with a "tough cowboy" persona. We'd been working together over many years, and we "got each other."

I shared my frustrating experience with him from my networking breakfast earlier. "Why am I always described as 'nice' and 'quiet'? Why can't people see me as 'fierce and strong'?"

He leaned across the boardroom table, looked me straight in the eye, and said in his gruff, gravelly, Clint Eastwood voice:

"Well, I guess you better sharpen your fangs!"

I laughed nervously and quickly refocused on the project at hand. *Fangs? Really?*

After a day filled with meetings, and feeling annoyed with rush hour traffic, I finally arrived home. My husband asked me how my day was, and I said, "Terrible…someone called me nice!"

He looked bewildered.

Okay, so I needed to put this in perspective, but there was so much more to me than just "nice."

A couple days later, I was sitting in my office, still unable to shake the feeling of disappointment. *Why don't they see the hardworking, pit-bull side of me? I've always been the smart, nice kid. I know because it's in all my report cards, and I remember the teachers always telling my parents how: "Laura plays nicely with others."*

Playground Badass

Even as a young child I was more than that—more than just "nice." In grade three, I remember playing marbles at recess on the asphalt compound of our Catholic school. Most of the kids played marbles in the spring, and I played too. I was good at it. I was shrewd, and I usually won. Playing marbles was like a market—there were "vendors" and "shoppers." The vendors set up marbles next to the brick wall and chanted their offering. "Hit one, get 'em all," was one I remembered. The "shoppers" strolled by the marble displays—and looked for the best set up, with the most opportunity to win more marbles.

Well, one day, as a "shopper," I browsed the market with my purple, Crown Royal bag, filled to the brim with my winnings. I walked up and down the vendors' displays and looked for the most enticing ones.

I passed by a tempting set up of marbles. The vendor was the tough guy of the school. His blond hair was shaved close to his head, and he always wore a dirty white T-shirt. He was a mean boy, a bully who I always avoided, but not that day. I wanted to shoot my marbles at his set up—as he had the best deal going, and I could win a lot of marbles. But I could see his large, center boulder was set in a divot in the asphalt. *I knew where all the divots were.* I wondered if he put it there to hide a chip.

"Is that marble chipped?" I asked him nicely.

"No," he said.

Just like I saw him as the tough guy at school, I am sure he saw me as the nice girl. He likely saw no challenge in dealing with me. He could say whatever he wanted, and I would play along, right? *Wrong.*

I confronted him on the suspected chipped rock before attempting to shoot my marbles.

"Are you sure that centre boulder doesn't have a chip on the bottom?" I asked firmly.

"No, it's fine," he said. But as I watched him, his eyes shifted, and then he twitched ever so slightly.

"Okay, then show me," I said defiantly.

After an intense nose-to-nose stand-off, he picked up the marble and showed me the bottom of it. Lo and behold, there was a deep chip in it. He looked at me and gulped—and I stared him in the eye, turned and walked away. I was not going to play with a cheater.

In my own mind (*and I think, his*), I became a badass that day.

Years later, I wondered why the bully always wore the same dirty clothes to school and sported unfashionably cropped hair for the time—and why no one ever taught him how to play marbles properly.

What was going on in his life at home that made him so angry and mean? Did anyone ever take the time to teach him how to play a game fair and square? Did he end up building a happy, productive life? I hope so.

Funeral Badass (well, sorta)

I couldn't seem to shake my client's comment that I need to "sharpen my fangs." Maybe I needed to show them more often—like I did at my mother's funeral.

After my mom had died from her lengthy struggle with COPD, my dad, siblings, and I gathered to plan her funeral. I proclaimed that I would like to give her eulogy. My brothers and sister agreed without hesitation. They certainly didn't want to do it, and I felt a really strong obligation—a yearning to write and deliver it.

I had started writing the eulogy, and I felt very confident in my theme and all the stories I had weaved into the tribute. In an odd way, the writing came very easily, and I felt I was getting help from a higher power as I typed the words.

A few days before the funeral, my sister-in-law phoned me late at night. She sounded a bit nervous, and then blurted out that I shouldn't do the eulogy. She said "Laura, you are just too shy and quiet. I think it might be too hard for you to stand up in front of all our family and friends and actually give a speech about your mother."

I don't think she said this to hurt me. I think she wanted to avoid any kind of embarrassment with me crumbling at the podium in a pool of tears.

While trying not to be argumentative, I confidently said, "No, I really want to do this. It's important to me."

She kindly urged me to reconsider. "I really think you should have someone else do it. This is the first parent to pass away in the family, and it will be an emotional day as it is. Giving the eulogy will add to your stress. I'm concerned that you may be too emotional to speak in front of a large crowd."

While she may have been right about this, the words stung a bit. *But the reality was, my mom had been dying for a very long time.* While her passing was incredibly sad, it wasn't a total surprise. And in an odd way, it was kind of a relief that Mom's pain and suffering was finally over. She could now rest in peace.

Stubbornly, I held my ground with my sister-in-law.

I knew I could give my mom a well-deserved send off.

And as I hung up the phone, I mumbled to myself, "*Just watch me.*"

At the funeral, I confidently rose to the podium in my dark blue suit and crisp white blouse, straightened my shoulders, and took a deep breath.

In a crowded Catholic church, with the priest sitting only a few feet from me, I centered my mother's eulogy around three things: Faith, Hope, and Charity.

Faith: I told the congregation that my mother didn't need the walls of a church to be a good Catholic—she rarely attended mass, but she was the most Christian person I knew.

Hope: When my dad had his heart attack, my mom knew that he was going to come home to her—and he did.

Charity: Mom had a few favourite charities that she regularly donated to, but she didn't brag about it. She gave where she could and kept it private—between her and God.

Finally, I told the congregation that you could never phone or visit Mom at 11:00 in the morning. *The Price is Right* was on, and you dared not interrupt her and Bob Barker.

And she was smart—oh, so smart. She could talk about pinch pleats or politics with the most riveting and lively discussions.

My mom was also tough. She was not the type to give you hugs and kisses, but the type that pushed you to be strong, fierce, and independent.

People were nodding and laughing and wiping away tears as I spoke. I made a connection with the audience, and I felt they looked up at me on that podium with admiration and love.

That was my badass eulogy. People came up to me afterwards and said it was the best eulogy they had ever heard.

I don't know where I got the theme of Faith, Hope, and Charity. It just entered my mind as I was typing her eulogy days before the funeral. Oddly enough (*being the perfectionist I am*), I thought I better look up Faith, Hope, and Charity because I referred to them as "virtues" in the eulogy, and I wanted to make sure that was correct. My research validated that they were, in fact, virtues. I also found out that "Faith, Hope, and Charity were sisters— and their mother was Saint Sophia."

My mother wasn't a Saint (*just a mere mortal*), but her name was Sophie.

This revelation sent a shiver down my spine. I had done good. My own faith and instincts to listen to my heart were spot on. While I didn't really show my fangs that day, they did get sharper.

Dance Floor Badass

Then I remembered the Red, Red, Wine moment.

It was my daughter's wedding day. A beautiful Saturday in August with the sun shining brightly—and the temperature was just right. My daughter had grown into a beautiful woman. She was tall and thin, with blonde hair and intense blue eyes. She was smart, vibrant, and popular—with exquisite, classic taste (*much like my mother*). For the big day, she chose a plain, fitted wedding dress—understated except for the white lace overlay which gave the dress texture and sheen. She contrasted it with a belt covered in pearls and crystals that drew the eye to her tiny waist. The gown was strapless and emphasized her strong arms and shoulders. An elaborate pearl and crystal necklace adorned her neck, and its detail highlighted the simplicity of the dress even more. Her thick, shiny hair was swept up in an elegant bun held in place by a clip—encrusted with pearls and crystals. From the clip, a long, white veil spilled from the nape of her neck to the satin-covered buttons perfectly aligned down her back. She wore her grandmother's aquamarine engagement ring on her right hand—a gift from her grandpa to his wife on their wedding day many years earlier in Italy. My daughter looked exquisite.

As the mother-of-the-bride, I chose a champagne-coloured knee-length cocktail dress. It was understated and demure. My shoes and purse matched my dress almost perfectly. I wore a champagne-coloured crystal necklace and earrings that my goddaughter had given me for Christmas the year before. Everything was seamlessly coordinated. The final touch to my polished look was sheer pantyhose that had a very delicate shimmer of gold. Most excitedly, they weren't control top, as I had recently lost a lot of weight for this big day. I felt good—and I felt strong.

The church ceremony, dinner, and cake-cutting went according to our meticulously laid plans. My husband and I both wrote speeches, and we were happily greeted with laughs where we hoped and tears where we shared poignant memories.

Later in the evening, the bride—always the centre of attention, started dancing to Taylor Swift's "Shake It Off." It wasn't long before she had the whole bridal party on the dance floor. In typical, "let's get this party started" fashion, she proceeded to climb onto the tabletop, in her ivory-coloured high heels and danced the hours away!

As the night wore on, the deejay started to play "Red, Red, Wine" by UB40. It is one of my favourites, so I immediately took to the dance floor—but not without first stopping by the bar and picking up three bottles of red wine. I proceeded to hand the bottles to a couple of the neighbourhood moms, and we danced through the song—more than once. By the end of it, red wine spilled onto the dance floor, and my expensive, gold shimmery pantyhose were sopping wet from dancing shoeless. It didn't matter. We were having fun. Soon, many of the moms—and even some of the grandmas were on the dancefloor with full bottles of wine in their hands.

It was crazy, and it was unexpected. My demure, mother-of-the-bride outfit was no more. I was waving my arms over my head and swinging my hips without any inhibitions. I couldn't have been happier.

But something even better was about to happen.

One of my daughter's friends came up to me as I exited the dance floor and said, "Now I know where the bride gets her personality. You were on the dance floor all night, drinking from a bottle of wine. **You are a Badass!!!**"

As I recounted these stories, I realized that being a badass doesn't mean you have to ride a Harley with black leather pants and a bandana. A badass is standing up to the bullies, defying the odds, and sometimes letting go of your inhibitions.

How does this story relate to art and design in our everyday lives? Well, constantly being described as "nice" made me realize that while *I am* nice, I am also quietly fierce. And that has translated to my work. My design skills have grown and developed through the years, and my quiet confidence has enabled me to become a better listener. It has made me a more empathic designer to my clients—truly understanding their challenges and goals. I have learned to ask good questions—important questions so that my designs and strategies serve them well.

Bottom line: Being quiet and nice has enabled me to be one badass designer!

Wrapping it Up with a Bow

Designing with Words

I have been working with a marketing associate for over twenty years, and she has become a dear friend of mine. We have been in many client meetings over that time, and she would always tease me when I ended each design pitch with "You have to wrap it up in a bow."

You see, I would preach to my clients that we could work with them to develop a strong brand—from the logo to the colour choices, imagery, and tone of the messaging. It had to be fluid and smooth and the quality, values, and experiences had to be consistent, and draped together in a beautifully presented package—bow and all.

So that is what I am going to do here. I am going to wrap this up in a bow.

I have had a book in me for decades. While I am normally fairly quiet, I often have something to say but usually can't get it out fast enough. Or rather, I'm not able to express myself the way I want to. But through my design career, I realized that part of my job was not only to present my ideas but to *sell* them to clients. Of course, it was imperative the designs were well-developed and properly executed with strong rationale to back them up. Being a good talker wasn't going to let me get away with subpar work. I found if I really thought through my designs—took good notes to understand my client's objectives and goals, and then circled back to review them as I worked—the foundation of my design choices became very clear. Usually, my hard work was quickly approved, and clients were ecstatic with the results. All that upfront thinking, more often than not, worked.

I Learned to Design

Questions—lots of questions—were essential. I'd review objectives, challenges, goals, and audiences to determine who, what, where, when, and why?

"Tell me more about your ideal client. Explain your selling process. Tell me how you fulfil your orders. How do you want your customers to *feel* about your brand?"

There was a constant barrage of questions to understand my clients' offerings as well as how they wanted their customers' journey to flow from beginning to end.

A design was rarely complete in one sitting. Daily interruptions, including phone calls, emails, and meetings, could be annoying when a deadline was looming, but were more than welcome when time was available. Upon each revisit of my work, there was an opportunity to reevaluate the design solution. *Hmm, too loud, too soft, too weak, too busy.* This process of revisiting a project again and again with fresh eyes and a fresh perspective, forced more critical thinking—which evolved into better work.

I Learned to Talk

As my career progressed, so did my ability to express myself verbally. But I still dreamed of merging artwork with written words. As a visual person, I always respected that "content was king." My designs framed and guided viewers through words. Merging the two was where the real magic happened.

As a young graduate from art college, I told my dad that I dreamed of writing children's books one day. With my art background and my sensitive nature, I had lots of ideas about storytelling in relation to children. My dear dad cut out every ad he came across that marketed to those who dreamed of writing for children. I looked at them— but rolled my eyes and discarded them quickly. Although I *wanted* to write a book, I wasn't a natural. I was trained in art and design. While I had this dream, it seemed quite impossible to think I would ever become a writer. But over the years, and with Dad's persistent ads tossed my way, I finally took a business-book writing workshop. Although my focus has changed from writing children's books, I hope to tackle that challenge as well someday.

I Learned How to Write

The business-book writing course started the fever in me. While I didn't want to write about *business* per se, I did want to write about something I knew—art and design.

I quickly found that writing with words was very similar to designing with images and typography. It was a matter of putting the right combination of letters, words, descriptions, and most importantly, *feelings* into everything I wrote. My writing coach frequently pushed me: "Show me; don't tell me." And that became my mantra.

Ahhhh, I knew how to "show" things. As a graphic designer, it was all about how things looked and how people reacted. Whether the design was a print ad, video, trade show booth, social media post, or even a website, I learned how to design persuasively. At a glance, my designs had to convey the essence of my client's offering—both visually and in conjunction with strong key messaging. I finally saw the parallel between writing with words and designing with them. My artistic mood board was now parlayed with a thesaurus.

Like choosing a colour palette for a design, setting the tone for a story started with painting a picture with words. What emotion did I want to evoke? How would I describe the character? What were the most honest adjectives I could choose to depict an image in a reader's mind? Much like selecting high contrast colours to design a hard-sell ad, or soft colours and lightweight typography to create calmness, the choice of words became critical to depicting what I wanted a story to *do*. While I was taught to use an exclamation mark judiciously, how else could I create urgency and excitement, or poetic symmetry with just words?

Just Words

I always knew how important words were, but I never realized how creative I could be with words alone. As a designer, my world expanded when I learned to write creatively. Up to this point, the only thing I had written were business proposals, schedules, and project plans.

I have discovered how to devote the same dedication to flowing words together as I do when fitting pixels together. Describing a situation is more than giving a step-by-step account. At one point, I thought that writing was to get to the point of your story quickly. I have since learned that writing with detailed dialogue, descriptions, and the proper tone resonate so much better with the audience.

A Different Kind of Journey

I have learned how to take the reader on a journey with my storytelling—hopefully enlightening them, making them laugh, or sharing an experience that evokes a different point of view. It is much like persuasive graphic design, where my job is to attract the viewer with strong imagery and then use copy to guide and entice them to take an action—whether that action is to email, call with questions, or make a purchase.

In merging the two disciplines (*and I call them disciplines because neither comes easily*), I am honing my craft—assimilating images with letters, words, messaging. And it's become a fascinating, colourful world where the visual and the written worlds unite in a powerfully creative way—and are beautifully wrapped up in a bow.

This one's for you, Dad. I hope there is a copy in Heaven, so you can curl up on a soft cloud and enjoy.

Epilogue

My Brand is Badass

"Brand" is used liberally today. It can represent both businesses and individuals. A personal brand is how one may describe and promote themselves as a person. Personal brands can be promoted through direct contacts at informal gatherings, as well as through social media, podcasts, and professional networking. A business brand is often how we identify and present our product and service offerings. Business branding may be more formal and broader, with promotion coming from advertising, social media channels, and traditional marketing. Both brand types should be wrapped in strong values, beliefs, and grit.

As a designer, I never imagined *I'd* be sharing my own personal brand so openly. After all, I have spent my entire career branding my clients—not me. However, breast cancer, in the odd way cancer works, gave me the confidence to share my vulnerable side. It made me stronger, forced me to dig deeper, and tugged at me to share stories throughout my cancer journey. Inspiring stories.

Here's just one:

After breast cancer, surgery, and subsequent tests, my oncologist decided that chemotherapy would also be part of my treatment (a massive surprise to me and my family).

I was devastated knowing my hair would fall out. It may sound vain, but my hair was the one thing I really coveted. However, other serious life events happened before my chemo started that put my hair loss into perspective.

A dear friend called me on a Sunday–Mother's Day, to be exact. This was the day before I was to start my chemotherapy. I thought she was calling to wish me luck. But I heard a panic in her voice and immediately knew something was wrong. She said she didn't want to share the news with me today, but she thought I should know.

Every weekend in the spring and summer, my friend would go to her holiday trailer, which was parked in a picturesque campground overlooking the foothills of Alberta. It was peaceful and filled with like-minded campers who enjoyed their weekends away from the big city. Her 30-minute door-to-door drive from house to trailer was scenic and typically carefree. However, on this routine drive, she had a car accident. Not just any car accident, however. It was a collision with a young man on his new motorcycle. She was making a left-hand turn on a typically quiet country road. There was a truck and cattle trailer ahead of her, making the same turn. She stopped and was waiting behind the long truck and trailer combo. Looking in her rearview mirror, she suddenly saw a motorbike driving very fast and realized he was not slowing down. To her horror, he hit her car and violently pushed her into the vehicle ahead. The velocity of the crash was enormous, and the results were unthinkable. Sadly, the young motorcyclist passed away at the scene.

As my friend recounted this excruciating, life-changing story, my chemotherapy treatment seemed like nothing in comparison. It was Mother's Day, and this young man's mom had to deal with his untimely death. There would be no card or visit from her beloved son that day—or any in the years to come.

There was nothing to compare to this loss of life.

I was completely devastated, but it gave me unexpected resolve for my upcoming chemo infusions. I was going to be okay. I dared to mourn the loss of my hair while a devastated mother was mourning the loss of her son. This dire accident put things in perspective very quickly.

My hair would grow back.

My perspective shifted dramatically after my friend's accident, and I saw things differently as a chemo patient…

Two and a half weeks into chemo, my hair started to fall out—just like the cancer pamphlet predicted. It was the May long weekend, and I was planting flower pots on the deck. I needed to have those flowers planted so I could watch them grow and blossom as I moved through my aggressive treatment plan.

There was a light breeze blowing as I planted each container. Several strands of hair fell from my head and landed in the flowers. The delicate petals and green leaves seemed to gently catch my hair and hold onto them. It was mesmerizing. As I watched my long tresses being caught in the plants, I thought, *I hope the birds come by and take this hair for their nests. It would be nice for them to build a home for their babies to rest in—with the hair I had loved so much.* Oddly, this gave me great comfort. It was like the circle of life I had come to appreciate from *The Lion King*.

As I moved through my cancer treatments, I noted the many brave women and men who paved the way for me, making my journey easier, including my dear friend in this story. I am documenting these inspiring stories from special people who have given me hope. I will share them as well as more of my own stories in *The Blue Garden Bench: Inspiring Stories of My Breast Cancer Journey*.

The subject matter may look a bit different from my first book, *The Green Velvet Chair*, which explores how we communicate through art in everyday life. But make no mistake, a journey through cancer diagnosis and treatment is about art and design as well.

From the artistic talents of a surgeon—whose medium is not clay but rather human flesh; to wig specialists and creative caregivers, I can attest to the fact that art and design are involved every step of the way.

Life is art.

My path is unwinding in a way I didn't expect, but I am embracing it. Sharing my vulnerability through my breast cancer journey, a strong sense of personal brand power has been born.

My inner badass has been unleashed.

References

Chapter 3 "Digging Deep in the Vatican Museum"

"Castel Gandolfo of Rome - Useful Information - Rome & Vatican Museums," Rome Museum (Italy Museum, accessed November 06, 2021), https://www.rome-museum.com/castel-gandolfo.php

"Lake Albano," Encyclopædia Britannica (Encyclopædia Britannica, Inc., July 20, 1998), https://www.britannica.com/place/Lake-Albano

"St. Peter's Basilica of Vatican City - Useful Information," Rome Museum (Italy Museum, accessed November 06, 2021), https://www.rome-museum.com/st-peters-basilica.php

P. Murray, "St. Peter's Basilica," Encyclopedia.com (Encyclopedia.com, 1998), https://www.encyclopedia.com/religion/encyclopedias-almanacs-transcripts-and-maps/st-peters-basilica

"Pietà," Michelangelo's Pietà (Michaelangelo.net, 2021), http://www.michelangelo.net/pieta/

Jimmy Kennedy, "The Gallery of the Tapestries," Vatican Tips (She Media, February 3, 2020), https://vaticantips.com/the-gallery-of-the-tapestries/

Chapter 4 "Follow the Bouncing Ball"

Gabby Hammond, "How the World Trade Center Sphere Traveled NYC after 9/11," 911 Ground Zero (Ground Zero Tours, September 18, 2020), https://911groundzero.com/blog/historic-koenig-sphere-returns-to-world-trade-center/

"The Sphere," Wikipedia (Wikimedia Foundation, October 28, 2021), https://en.wikipedia.org/wiki/The_Sphere#:~:text=The%20largest%20bronze%20sculpture%20of,Landshut%2C%20where%20Fritz%20Koenig%20lived

"The Sphere, a Symbol of Resilience and Survival, Rededicated in Liberty Park," 9/11 Memorial and Museum (National September 11 Memorial & Museum, 2021), https://www.911memorial.org/connect/blog/sphere-symbol-resilience-and-survival-rededicated-liberty-park

"World Trade Center Site Memorial Competition," Wikipedia (Wikimedia Foundation, September 12, 2021), https://en.wikipedia.org/wiki/World_Trade_Center_Site_Memorial_Competition

"Rescue and Recovery Effort after the September 11 Attacks on the World Trade Center," Wikipedia (Wikimedia Foundation, September 27, 2021), https://en.wikipedia.org/wiki/Rescue_and_recovery_effort_after_the_September_11_attacks_on_the_World_Trade_Center

Mary Kay Linge, "9/11 Survivor Trees a Symbol of Hope and Resilience across the World," New York Post (New York Post, September 10, 2021), https://nypost.com/2021/09/11/9-11-survivor-trees-a-symbol-of-hope-and-resilience-across-the-world/

Hargittai István and Magdolna Hargittai, New York Scientific: A Culture of Inquiry, Knowledge, and Learning (Oxford, United Kingdom: Oxford University Press, 2017), 264.

Chapter 5 "Grace in Graceland"

Jordan Runtagh, "Paul Simon's 'Graceland': 10 Things You Didn't Know," Rolling Stone (Rolling Stone, September 22, 2019), https://www.rollingstone.com/feature/paul-simons-graceland-10-things-you-didnt-know-105220/

"Graceland (Album)," Wikipedia (Wikimedia Foundation, October 18, 2021), https://en.wikipedia.org/wiki/Graceland_(album)

Robin Denselow, "Paul Simon's Graceland: The Acclaim and the Outrage," The Guardian (Guardian News and Media, April 19, 2012), https://www.theguardian.com/music/2012/apr/19/paul-simon-graceland-acclaim-outrage

"Tour Graceland Mansion," Graceland (Graceland/Elvis Presley Enterprises Inc., accessed November 06, 2021), https://www.graceland.com/mansion

"Sun Studio," Wikipedia (Wikimedia Foundation, October 24, 2021), https://en.wikipedia.org/wiki/Sun_Studio

"Sam Phillips," Sun Record Company (Sun Entertainment Corporation, July 16, 2017), https://www.sunrecords.com/artists/sam-phillips

"Memphis, Tennessee," Wikipedia (Wikimedia Foundation, October 27, 2021), https://en.wikipedia.org/wiki/Memphis,_Tennessee

"Inside the Abandoned in Memphis, Tennessee Wonder Bread Factory," Autopsy of Architecture (Autopsy of Architecture, July 29, 2020), https://autopsyofarchitecture.com/wonder-bread-factory/

"The Hermitage Hotel - Luxury Hotels in Downtown Nashville TN," The Hermitage Hotel (The Hermitage Hotel, accessed November 06, 2021), https://www.thehermitagehotel.com/

Marc Cohn, "Marc Cohn – Walking in Memphis," ed. Sadchild and Young Cocoa Butter, Genius (Genius Media Group, 2021), https://genius.com/Marc-cohn-walking-in-memphis-lyrics

Allyson Hobbs, "The Lorraine Motel and Martin Luther King," The New Yorker (The New Yorker, January 18, 2016), https://www.newyorker.com/news/news-desk/the-lorraine-motel-and-martin-luther-king

James V Roy, "The Shure 55s: The 'Elvis Mic,'" Scotty Moore (James V. Roy, 2014), http://www.scottymoore.net/shure55s.html

Robby Moss, "Rendezvous Ribs: A Memphis Barbecue Tradition," Southern Living (Meredith Corporation, 2021), https://www.southernliving.com/souths-best/charlie-vergos-rendezvous-memphis-bbq

Charles Hughes, "The Man Who Brought Down Racial Barriers through Music," The Washington Post (WP Company, November 20, 2015), https://www.washingtonpost.com/opinions/the-man-who-brought-down-racial-barriers-through-music/2015/11/20/b34aa078-870c-11e5-be8b-1ae2e4f50f76_story.html

Chapter 6 "Makin" the Dough"

Cydney Grannan, "Why Is Saffron so Expensive?," Encyclopædia Britannica (Encyclopædia Britannica, inc., accessed November 06, 2021), https://www.britannica.com/story/why-is-saffron-so-expensive#:~:text=Since%20such%20a%20small%20part,to%20saffron's%20being%20majorly%20expensive

Chapter 8 "The Munster Mash"

"The Munsters," TV Tropes (TV Tropes, accessed November 06, 2021), https://tvtropes.org/pmwiki/pmwiki.php/Series/TheMunsters

"Teenage Mutant Ninja Turtles," Wikipedia (Wikimedia Foundation, November 3, 2021), https://en.wikipedia.org/wiki/Teenage_Mutant_Ninja_Turtles

"Spider-Man," Wikipedia (Wikimedia Foundation, November 4, 2021), https://en.wikipedia.org/wiki/Spider-Man

"Paul Stanley," Wikipedia (Wikimedia Foundation, November 4, 2021), https://en.wikipedia.org/wiki/Paul_Stanley

Hadley Meares, "Why Royal Women Gave Birth in Front of Huge Crowds for Centuries," History.com (A&E Television Networks, April 19, 2019), https://www.history.com/news/royal-birth-traditions-marie-antoinette-meghan-markle

"Louis XIV: 'The Sweetest-Smelling King of All'," The Perfume Society (Perfume Society, September 12, 2018), https://perfumesociety.org/history/louis-xiv-the-sweetest-smelling-king-of-all/

Lauren Marie, "False Hips and What Not," Marie Antoinette's Gossip Guide to the 18th Century (Lauren Marie, accessed November 06, 2021), https://www.mariegossip.com/2009/11/false-hips-and-what-not.html

"The Orangery," Chateau de Versailles (Chateau de Versailles, June 12, 2019), https://en.chateauversailles.fr/discover/estate/gardens/orangery

Chapter 9 "From Mouse to House"

"Women's Scarves and Silk Accessories," Hermés Paris (Hermés, 2021), https://www.hermes.com/ca/en/category/women/scarves-and-silk-accessories/?gclid=CjwKCAjwqe WKBhBFEiwABo_XBrJ-b4tcJ0mPHhcupAB8q3Sr2cxY1lMQy6KzFtvvGmtfm9N7InBkCBo CezYQAvD_BwE#|||Material

Chapter 10 "A Cat's Perspective"

Raybould, Barry John. "Atmospheric Perspective - Creating Mood and Feeling in the Landscape." Virtual Art Academy (Virtual Art Academy, September 17, 2021), https://www.virtualartacademy.com/atmospheric-perspective/#:~:text=Atmospheric%20 perspective%20refers%20to%20the,in%20value%2C%20saturation%20and%20 hue.&text=Atmospheric%20perspective%20is%20also%20called%20aerial%20perspective

Chapter 12 "A Brand Runs Deep"

"Flashdance," Wikipedia (Wikimedia Foundation, October 25, 2021), https://en.wikipedia.org/wiki/Flashdance

Chapter 16 "Designer Genes"

https://www.sciencealert.com/heres-how-events-in-your-grandparents-lives-could-affect-your-genes

https://www.bps.org.uk/psychologist/what-makes-great-art

https://spotlight.leeds.ac.uk/research-journeys-you-are-what-your-grandmother-ate/index.html#:~:text=To%20explain%20the%20story%20from,life%20in%20our%20 grandmothers'%20wombs.

https://www.fertilityanswers.com/the-incredible-human-egg/#:~:text=It%20is%20 believed%20that%20a,she%20was%20inside%20your%20grandmother!

Acknowledgements

I feel like I'm writing an Oscar speech as I have so many people to thank and don't want to forget anyone.

First of all, I would like to express my gratitude to my Oral Storytelling Coach, Adele Fedorak. Without her encouragement and push to "use my voice," this book would never have happened. Thank you, Adele, for believing in me, challenging me, and inspiring me to find and nurture my inner badass. *I actually didn't even know I had one until we started working together.*

Adele introduced me to the one-and-only Kathy Sparrow—literary midwife and publishing consultant. Thank you, Kathy for your guidance, depth of knowledge, and empathy. This was both an academic and emotional journey and you were there to support me, not only through the edits but through the laughter and deep conversations around the stories. You made me believe that I could not only write—but that I could write well. And thanks for guiding me through this 2nd Edition.

A special thank you to Kimberlee Jones for writing the Foreword for this book. I have known Kim for many decades and appreciate her thoughtful and creative writing skills, as well as her continued support on this project.

Beta readers: without you and your candid, sensitive feedback, many aspects of the stories would not be as rich as they now are. Your honesty and constructive critiques, mixed in with a few tears kept me going. Each of you validated that I had something of value to say—and you helped me say it better. Thank you to Allison McGee, Arlene Mankowski, Brenda Sevick, Caran Magaw, Dana Goldstein, Jane Coates, Jeff Nelson, Jill Curry, Kimberlee Jones, Len Edwards, Lindsay Walters, Pam Boytinck, and Rita Lisella.

Finally, I want to thank my family watching this at home (*tee hee*). This book was all-consuming, and you patiently supported me and indulged me when I once again reread a new version of a chapter to you. Kimberly, your wise art direction made the stories varied, yet consistent. Cheryl, your reviews and spot-on comments kept me on my toes. And George, well what can I say? Your constant support and encouragement every day is more than I could ever have wanted. Cooking dinner and doing the dishes while I toiled at the computer supported me in ways that only you would have known. Thank you all.

This experience has been so rewarding, and I owe much of it to each and every one of you.

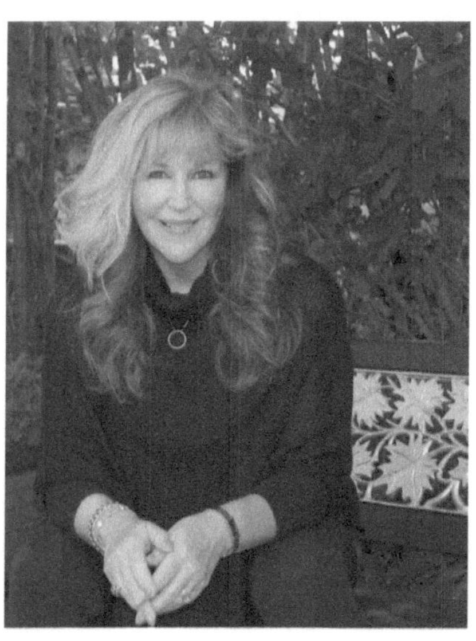

About the Author

Laura Ballerini is a seasoned graphic designer with a degree in Visual Communications and over forty years of working in the industry. Ballerini has experienced the many facets of art, design and communications over the decades. Having worked for a big-city newspaper, a leading Advertising Agency, and currently running her own design boutique, BluBrown Communications Inc., Laura has honed her skills to merge writing and visual design into one. *BluBrown is named after her two daughters—one with blue eyes and one with brown eyes; the concept was to always look at design through the fresh eyes of a child—and always ask "why?"*

Laura lives in Calgary, Alberta, with her husband, two daughters, one son-in-law, a granddaughter, and a pretentious cat named Gooey.

The Green Velvet Chair is Laura's first book.

Contact Info: **LBallerini@BluBrown.com**

Questions and Topics for Discussion

Chapter 1: From Picas to Pixels

- Have you had any colourful, "larger than life" characters in your life? If so, describe them. Have any of them gone on to fame and glory? What is your definition of "fame and glory"?

- Have you experienced camaraderie with your work associates, or a personal group of friends? Please describe.

- Do you see your life transitioning to something completely different in twenty years? If so, explain.

- Are you conscious of the growth throughout your personal and/or professional life? If so, what does it feel like? (Painful, scary, fun, exciting, easy, etc.?)

Chapter 2: Watching my Mother Through the Smoke

- Have you ever watched someone suffer from illness or disease?

- Has anyone ever inspired you in your life? If so, who? Describe them and how they inspired you.

- Do you have a favourite holiday tradition? Describe.

- Did you ever feel frustrated with the gender you were born in to? (Did it hold you back or help you?)

- Has someone ever shared their vision with you (whatever it may be)? Did you envision it too, or was it impossible to "see"?

- How would you like to be remembered? (Inspiring, kind, strong, other?) Explain.

Chapter 3: Digging Deep in the Vatican Museum

- Have you ever travelled with a group of people you've never met? What was it like?

- Did you ever feel others were holding you back or slowing you down? How did you handle/overcome the situation?

- Describe a moment where you experienced a different culture from your own that was life changing.

- Have you ever looked at a piece of artwork and wondered, how did that become "art"?

- Has art (in any form) ever made you feel happy, sad, angry, or upset? How and why?

- Did it change your point of view?

Chapter 4: Follow the Bouncing Ball

- Did you ever experience something (art, person, event), and it seemed to repeatedly show up in your life at various times?

- Have you ever experienced a traumatic event and needed to retell it again and again (almost as if helping you understand and cope with it better)?

- Is there a particular artist or person who has influenced you in your life, or your work?

- Has artwork ever moved you to tears? Explain what and why.

Chapter 5: Grace in Graceland

- Have you ever been influenced by music? How, why, when?
- Do you, or have you ever played a musical instrument? Explain.
- Have you ever been surprised by the origins of a song's lyrics and what they really meant when the artist wrote them?
- Have you ever experienced culture shock? Explain where and when. How did you deal with it?
- What was your favourite lunch as a kid? Do you have sentimental memories of it?

Chapter 6: Making the Dough

- Do you have a special family dish that you prepare for special events? (Easter, Christmas, birthdays, etc.)
- Have you ever thought of cooking and/or baking as a form of art? Explain.
- Do you have a family recipe that was passed down through the generations? Describe.
- Have you found modern ingredients and processes have changed the taste of a dish, even if you followed the recipe exactly? Please describe.

Chapter 7: COVID-19: The Year My Mother-in-Law Died

- COVID-19 had made 2020 a tough year for all of us. Did you experience loss? Please describe.
- Have you ever had a loved one move to a new residence to later regret the move? Describe.
- Have you ever experienced a "mean girl" (mean person) moment? When and what?
- Do you appreciate the stories from family members and friends? Do you try to preserve them for future generations? If so, how?
- Funerals are a solemn time, but have you ever experienced a funny (positive) moment during this sad time?

Chapter 8: The Munster Mash

- Do you have a favourite Halloween memory? Explain
- Do you see costume and make-up as forms of art? Please elaborate?
- Did you ever try to impress your boss? If so, how? Did it work?
- What was the best party you ever went to and why?
- Did you ever feel overlooked when you did all the work, but others got the recognition? Explain.

Chapter 9: From Mouse to House

- Online shopping is more prevalent than ever. Have you ever had a bad online purchasing experience? Explain.
- What aspects of a website tell you it's safe and trustworthy to use? Have you ever been disappointed?
- If you could buy anything for yourself, what would it be and why?
- Has someone ever surprised you with an extravagant, over the top gift? If so, how did you react? Describe.
- Do you prefer some brands over others? Why?

Chapter 10: A Cat's Perspective

- Have you ever seen a pet display strange behaviour? If so, please explain.
- Do you sometimes feel you are not getting the full story? If so, do you dig for more info or let it go? Describe.
- Do you form opinions based on one source of information, or do you strive to gain different perspectives and more clarity? Explain.
- The source of information is critical. Do you verify sources? Explain.
- How do you express your opinions in today's complex world without hurting or offending others?

Chapter 11: Every Picture Tells a Story

- Have you ever experienced a life-changing moment only to forget about it as time passes?
- Have you ever created a deep bond with a complete stranger? Explain.
- Has someone ever saved your life, or someone close to you? If so, who? Elaborate?
- Do you have a specific photo that sparks an important memory? Describe.
- Do you place any important pieces of art (photos, mementos) in special places in your home so you can appreciate them daily?

Chapter 12: A Brand Runs Deep

- Did you enjoy high school? Was it a positive experience? Explain.
- Did you ever wish you were someone else?
- Have you ever tried to prove yourself to others?
- Has someone ever told you how they never would have recognized you today? How did this make you feel? Describe.
- How important is your outward appearance to the overall essence of who you are as a person?

Chapter 13: Seeing Scarlett

- Many of us appreciate the wisdom of our elders. But do you value the insight of those younger than you? Why or why not?
- Do you take note of the colour of a person's eyes? Or do you see beyond the colour?
- Blending family life with work life is a juggling act. Do you have any insight to share?
- Is there one particular person who makes your life brighter every day? Describe.
- Did you ever forget about something, only to have someone else's appreciation of it make it valuable again?

Chapter 14: I'm Sew in Love with Barbie

- Growing up in the 60s was a unique decade with lots of social unrest, but it was also called "The Age of Innocence." What societal aspects of growing up in your era were unique to you? How did they mold you into who you are today?
- Did you have a particular toy that impacted you in your childhood? What was it, and how did it affect you?
- Is that toy still around, and does its brand still impact the world today? (i.e. Lego, Rubik's Cube, Hot Wheels, etc.)
- Do you have hobbies or passions that were triggered by your childhood? What are they, and how do they make you better because of them?

Chapter 15: A Day at the Museum

- Do you have special memories of a family member who made you feel extra special? If so, who were they, and what did they do?

- Has anyone ever introduced you to something that changed your life, such as art, sports, public service, etc.?

- Do common interests attract you to others? Or are you attracted to those who are very different from you, and why?

- Have you ever been unfairly judged by your age, gender, or ethnicity and chastised for something you didn't do? If so, how did you deal with it?

- Have you ever approached an adversary and worked with them to create a harmonious relationship? What did you do? What worked? What didn't work?

Chapter 16: Designer Genes

- Do you have someone special in your life who seems to be influenced by you? If so, do you feel pressure to be a good role model for them?

- Do you believe any of our personal traits are passed on from one generation to the next? If so, please describe.

- Do you find some family members are easier to connect with than others? If so, why?

- The "Grandma Egg Theory" is talked about in this chapter. Does it seem plausible? Why or why not?

Chapter 17: One Red Crayon

- Did you have a favourite teacher in school? What made them special?

- Did you ever forget to do your homework (at work or school)? If so, how did you feel? What was the outcome?

- Were you ever in a sticky situation where you had to get really creative to solve a problem? Describe.

- Was there ever an instance in your life where the outcome was greater and more positive than you could ever have imagined? Explain.

- Is there a life lesson from your childhood that sticks with you today? Describe.

Chapter 18: Designing in the Dirt

- Did you have a favourite summer job as a young adult? Describe and explain why.

- Did you acquire skills from a job years ago that you still use today? Describe.

- Is there a particular hobby that you love but wish you were better at it?

- Have you ever had a challenge that you couldn't overcome, and then figured out a "work around" to it?

- Do you find the more you access your creativity, the more ideas you produce?

Chapter 19: *When I Grow Up, I Want to be a Wedding Planner*

- Do you ever aim for perfection even though you know its unattainable? How does it make you feel?
- Have you ever found it hard to understand someone else's vision for a project that you were involved in? How did you handle it? What did you do?
- Did you ever find yourself getting caught up in the details and forgetting about the big picture?
- Were you ever in charge of a project and didn't trust your team members to follow through? How did you resolve it? What was the outcome?
- Have you ever planned an event and wished you had done things differently? If so, please describe.

Chapter 20: *Finding My Inner Badass*

- Have you ever felt invisible and unrecognized? If so, did it you make you more assertive—or withdrawn—and why?
- Have you had your own badass moment? Describe it.
- How can you find and nurture your inner badass on a regular basis?
- What brings out your inner badass?
- Did you ever wish someone else would find their inner badass? Describe.

Chapter 21: *Wrap It Up in a Bow*

- What is your style? Are you able to be spontaneous and decisive, or do you have to plan and rationalize each decision you make? Neither is right or wrong, just a personal style. Describe yours.
- Do you see more value in being the listener or the talker? Why?
- Have you had goals that you have strived to achieve? Did they change and evolve through the years?
- Was there an influential person in your life that encouraged you to follow your dreams? Who are they? How did they encourage you?